Great Medical Discoveries

Chemotherapy

by Sudipta Bardhan-Quallen

THOMSON

GALE

San Diego • Detroit • New York • San Francisco • Cleveland • New Haven, Conn. • Waterville, Maine • London • Munich

THOMSON
———✳———
GALE

© 2004 by Lucent Books. Lucent Books is an imprint of The Gale Group, Inc.,
a division of Thomson Learning, Inc.

For more information, contact
Lucent Books
27500 Drake Rd.
Farmington Hills, MI 48331-3535
Or you can visit our Internet site at http://www.gale.com

LIBRARY OF CONGRESS CATALOGING-IN-PUBLICATION DATA

Bardhan-Quallen, Sudipta.
   Chemotherapy / by Sudipta Bardhan-Quallen.
     p. cm. — (Great medical discoveries)
Summary: Discusses the impact of chemotherapy as a treatment for cancer, its history
and development, challenges it presents, and future research.
Includes bibliographical references and index.
   ISBN 1-56006-926-0 (hardback : alk. paper)
   1. Chemotherapy—Juvenile literature. [1. Chemotherapy. 2. Cancer—Chemotherapy.] I.
Title. II. Series.
RM263.B36 2004
616.99'4061—dc21
                                                2003009592

Printed in the United States of America

CONTENTS

FOREWORD

Throughout history, people have struggled to understand and conquer the diseases and physical ailments that plague us. Once in a while, a discovery has changed the course of medicine and sometimes, the course of history itself. The stories of these discoveries have many elements in common—accidental findings, sudden insights, human dedication, and most of all, powerful results. Many illnesses that in the past were essentially a death warrant for their sufferers are today curable or even virtually extinct. And exciting new directions in medicine promise a future in which the building blocks of human life itself—the genes—may be manipulated and altered to restore health or to prevent disease from occurring in the first place.

It has been said that an insight is simply a rearrangement of already-known facts, and as often as not, these great medical discoveries have resulted partly from a reexamination of earlier efforts in light of new knowledge. Nineteenth-century monk Gregor Mendel experimented with pea plants for years, quietly unlocking the mysteries of genetics. However, the importance of his findings went unnoticed until three separate scientists, studying cell division with a newly improved invention called a microscope, rediscovered his work decades after his death. French doctor Jean-Antoine Villemin's experiments with rabbits proved that tuberculosis was contagious, but his conclusions were politely ignored by the medical community until another doctor, Robert Koch of Germany, discovered the exact culprit—the tubercle bacillus germ—years later.

Accident, too, has played a part in some medical discoveries. Because the tuberculosis germ does not stain with dye as easily as other bacteria, Koch was able to see it only after he had let a treated slide sit far longer than he intended. An unwanted speck of mold led Englishman Alexander Fleming to recognize the bacteria-killing qualities of the penicillium fungi, ushering in the era of antibiotic "miracle drugs."

That researchers sometimes benefited from fortuitous accidents does not mean that they were bumbling amateurs who relied solely on luck. They were dedicated scientists whose work created the conditions under which such lucky events could occur; many sacrificed years of their lives to observation and experimentation. Sometimes the price they paid was higher. Rene Launnec, who invented the stethoscope to help him study the effects of tuberculosis, himself succumbed to the disease.

And humanity has benefited from these scientists' efforts. The formerly terrifying disease of smallpox has been eliminated from the face of the earth—the only case of the complete conquest of a once deadly disease. Tuberculosis, perhaps the oldest disease known to humans and certainly one of its most prolific killers, has been essentially wiped out in some parts of the world. Genetically engineered insulin is a godsend to countless diabetics who are allergic to the animal insulin that has traditionally been used to help them.

Despite such triumphs there are few unequivocal success stories in the history of great medical discoveries. New strains of tuberculosis are proving to be resistant to the antibiotics originally developed to treat them, raising the specter of a resurgence of the disease that has killed 2 billion people over the course of human history. But medical research continues on numerous fronts and will no doubt lead to still undreamed-of advancements in the future.

Each volume in the Great Medical Discoveries series tells the story of one great medical breakthrough—the first gropings for understanding, the pieces that came together and how, and the immediate and longer-term results. Part science and part social history, the series explains some of the key findings that have shaped modern medicine and relieved untold human suffering. Numerous primary and secondary source quotations enhance the text and bring to life all the drama of scientific discovery. Sidebars highlight personalities and convey personal stories. The series also discusses the future of each medical discovery—a future in which vaccines may guard against AIDS, gene therapy may eliminate cancer, and other as-yet unimagined treatments may become commonplace.

INTRODUCTION

Ancient Hopes, Modern Miracles

Chemotherapy is one of medicine's most potent weapons against an ancient scourge called cancer. Such weapons are in high demand, since cancer claims so many lives every year. In fact, cancer is the second leading cause of death among Americans; only heart disease takes more lives. According to the American Cancer Society, half of all men and one-third of all women in the United States will develop some form of cancer in their lifetimes. That translates to more than 1.3 million new cases of cancer diagnosed in 2002 alone, with more than half a million American cancer deaths in that same year.

The fight against cancer is, however, also a medical success story. In the early 1900s, an individual had almost no chance of surviving five years after receiving the initial cancer diagnosis. Thanks to the development of various treatments—including chemotherapy—by the 1940s the five-year survival rate improved to about 25 percent. At the turn of the twenty-first century, the majority of people diagnosed with cancer are likely to survive their battle against the disease; the five-year survival rate now stands at more than 60 percent.

Advances in chemotherapy have been largely responsible for this improvement. In the last century, chemotherapy has evolved from folk remedies to genetically engineered viruses targeting cancer cells on a molecular level. The search for chemotherapy drugs has shifted from looking for chemicals that could kill cancer cells, irrespective of the potential damage to healthy tissue, to designing highly specific drugs attuned to the genetic abnormalities of cancer cells alone.

A Formidable Weapon

Technically, chemotherapy includes everything from taking an aspirin for a headache to taking antitumor medications for breast cancer. The word chemotherapy literally means chemical therapy, so it can refer to any type of medical treatment that involves the administration of drugs. However, for practical purposes chemotherapy generally refers to the treatment of cancer with various drugs and chemical compounds.

Chemotherapy may be used alone or in concert with other types of treatment. In the beginning stages of cancer, when a tumor is small and localized, doctors will

Chemotherapy, the use of drugs and chemical compounds to treat disease, is one of the most powerful weapons against cancer.

often attempt to eliminate the tumor with surgery or radiation. These primary treatments destroy the vast majority of the cancer cells, then doctors prescribe chemotherapy, which kills any cancer cells that might remain behind. This combination helps ensure that the patient stays cancer-free. Sometimes chemotherapy is administered prior to the surgery or radiation. The goal in such cases is to shrink a tumor before other treatments are undertaken. In the most advanced cases, when the tumor has metastasized, or spread, the amount of surgery that would be needed to remove all the cancerous tissue would be too harmful to the patient. Doctors can use radiation for metastatic cancer, but at the high levels required, it often has unacceptably severe side effects; in fact, exposure to X-rays in high doses can actually cause cancer.

When cancer has spread to different parts of the body, chemotherapy is often the only real choice. Treatments range from one of the traditional drugs, which are injected into the bloodstream and almost guaranteed to reach every cell, whether cancerous or normal, to cutting-edge treatments that target cancer cells on a molecular level and seek out individual diseased cells only. No matter what regimen is ultimately selected, a cancer patient is very likely to undergo some type of chemotherapy.

In fact, studies suggest that it is only in very rare instances that a cancer patient can completely beat the disease without chemotherapy.

The range of options in chemotherapy is ever-expanding. As of 2002 more than four hundred chemotherapy drugs aimed at treating more than thirty different forms of cancer were available in the United States. As chemotherapy moves into a new millennium, greater attention is being paid to those approaches that will both prolong life and increase the quality of life of cancer patients. The future of chemotherapy is closely linked to research into the molecular events that occur when a cell becomes cancerous. Scientists

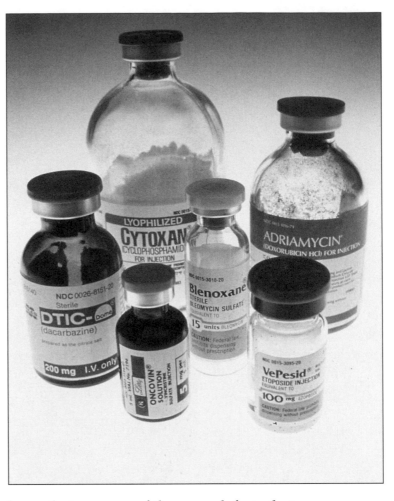

With greater under-standing of the gene defects that cause can-cer, researchers hope to develop new drugs that target unhealthy cells exclusively.

hope that as more of the gene defects that cause cancer are identified, drugs can be designed to impact only unhealthy cells. As other tumor-promoting processes are better understood, doctors can develop drugs to block those processes to better treat victims of this disease.

CHAPTER 1

The Search for a Magic Bullet

Since before recorded history, cancer has been a part of human life—and death. Long before humans understood why cancer occurred or how it killed, they recognized this disease. Humans also searched for ways to fight back, often using what might be called crude forms of chemotherapy. For example, in ancient China, people ate the Reishi mushroom when they suspected they suffered from stomach cancer. Other remedies ranged from the ancient Babylonians applying plasters of donkey dung to drinking ginger teas in ancient India. Only in the last century, however, have scientists methodically experimented with chemical cures for this disease.

A Five-Thousand-Year-Old Problem

One of the first people to describe a case of cancer was Imhotep, who in addition to being a royal adviser to the king of Egypt and an architect of the pyramids, was a talented physician. Beginning around 2600 B.C., in several papyrus scrolls, he extensively documented cases of cancer. In his descriptions, Imhotep did not call the ulcers and hard masses beneath the skin cancer, but the symptoms he noted were highly consistent with cancer. Imhotep's writings include references to lesions of the stomach, breast, uterus and skin. In addition to describing these lesions, Imhotep and other physicians in ancient Egypt differentiated between

11

benign tumors (those that do not grow out of control and spread) and malignant tumors (those that spread to other parts of the body).

Surgery was often used to remove malignant tumors, and the Egyptians were remarkably skilled at these types of surgeries. The physician would administer an anesthetic such as opium or belladonna to dull the pain of the procedure. The incisions were made with heated scalpels to minimize the risk of infection. Although the physician would be careful to avoid damaging any blood vessels during the surgery, he was always prepared to cauterize the wound—that is, seal it using heat—in case of a sudden hemorrhage. Depending on the type of tumor, it was either cut open and drained with the help of a hollow reed or removed in its entirety.

As skilled as the ancient Egyptians were at treating tumors surgically, they also often used naturally occurring substances to fight cancer. For example, to fight tumor growth, they ingested powders made from ground-up pig's ears mixed with barley, smeared pastes containing arsenic on the skin, or drank castor oil. Many of the substances they used contained active chemicals that really did have medicinal value, although the Egyptians did not fully understand the underlying chemistry or even what parts of their complex regimens were effective.

Early Remedies

Nonsurgical remedies continued to be popular in the search for a cure for cancer. In ancient Greece, a type of gingerroot called galangal was used to make a paste that could topically treat skin cancer. The Romans used a plant called red clover in an herbal tea, which when drunk would slow the growth of some tumors. Other cancers were treated by eating an extract from the autumn crocus. In the Far East, the ancient Chinese dissolved an herb called sweet wormwood in water to make an antitumor drink. In ancient India, a paste of turmeric was spread over the skin to treat, and perhaps even protect against, skin cancer.

Physicians, as described by the ancient Egyptians, continued to use arsenic to treat cancer, and the treatment's popularity peaked between the eleventh century in the Arabic world and the sixteenth century in Europe under the name *Unguentum Aegypticum* (literally, Egyptian unguent, or salve). These therapies varied in their effectiveness against cancer, but they were used when other treatments could not help the patient.

Early Descriptions and Treatments

Hippocrates coined the term carcinoma to describe cancer around 400 B.C. He noticed that tumors looked a little bit like *karkinoma*, the Greek word for crab. He described the center of the tumor as the body of the crab and noticed that the central tumor tended to have extensions that reached out of the center like the arms of a crab.

Hippocrates studied many different types of cancer including those of the breast, stomach, and uterus. While herbal remedies were available and widely used against cancer, Hippocrates concluded that cancerous tumors were best left untreated. He writes: "It is better not to apply any treatment

in cases of occult cancer; for, if treated, the patients die quickly; but if not treated, they hold out for a long time." Regardless of the efficacy of crude chemotherapy treatments, Hippocrates and the doctors of his age denounced the practice altogether.

The ancient Greek physician Hippocrates believed that cancerous tumors were best left untreated.

An Unpopular Alternative

Crude herbal and chemical treatments such as ginger and arsenic were frequently observed to be effective against cancer. Despite this success, doctors generally contended that cancer was best treated by surgery or left completely alone. In 1767 a scientist summarized the prevailing views on the use of medicines to cure cancer:

> Whatever has been proposed for the curing of cancers, are merely palliative medicines; and that no real specific has been hitherto discovered for that fatal disorder, although the physicians of all nations, from the time of Hippocrates to the present, have, by numberless researches and experiments, made trial of every thing in nature, from the most innocent drug, to the most virulent poison, both in the mineral and vegetable kingdoms; yet the disease still baffles.[1]

In other words, medicines might help cancer patients feel better but could not cure the disease. More than a hundred years later, in 1914, the American physician William Bainbridge echoed these sentiments:

> Throughout the centuries, the sufferers of this disease [cancer] have been the subject of almost every conceivable form of experimentation. The fields and forests, the apothecary shop and temple have been ransacked for some successful means of relief from the intractable malady. Hardly any animal had escaped making its contribution to hide or hair, tooth or toenail, thymus or thyroid, liver or spleen, in the vain search for a means of relief.[2]

Physicians seemed to view chemical remedies for cancer as charades that offered false hope to desperate people, even though such treatments had been in use for more than five millennia.

Surgery, however, was not a pleasant prospect for most cancer patients. Although surgeons could remove small, superficial tumors with minimal risk, surgery for large tumors or metastasized cancers was extremely traumatic for the patient. In the seventeeth century, for example, German surgeon Johann Scultetus treat-

A Study of Cancer

During the 1400s and 1500s doctors began to explore human anatomy through autopsy. They were particularly interested in describing anomalies (differences from normal, healthy conditions) such as the effects of cancer on the body. Antonio Benivieni was a Florentine physician who kept detailed records of the autopsies he performed. He published *De Abditis Nonnulus ac Mirandis Morborum et Sanationum Causis (On the Several Hidden and Strange Causes of Disease and Cure)* in 1507, in which he describes a case of carcinoma of the stomach. Michael Shimkin, in his book *Contrary to Nature*, quotes Benivieni:

My kinsman, Antonio Bruno, retained the food he had eaten for too short a time, and then threw it up undigested. . . . His body wasted away through lack of nourishment till little more than skin and bone remained. At last he was brought to his death. The body was cut open for reasons of public welfare. It was found that the opening of his stomach had closed up and it had hardened . . . with the result that nothing could pass through to the organs beyond, and death inevitably followed.

ed his breast cancer patients by completely removing the diseased breast. This process was extremely crude and painful. He would begin by attaching heavy cords to large needles that would pierce the base of the breast. He would pull on the cords while he cut the breast tissue away with a knife to remove the breast in one piece. Lastly, he cauterized the wound to stanch the bleeding. The death rate from infection and other complications following these kinds of surgeries probably approached the death rate from the cancer itself.

Trying Everything

Regardless of the opinions of most physicians, people continued to turn to nonsurgical alternatives to treat cancer. In the latter part of the nineteenth century, cancer patients tried everything from blood transfusions to oxygen therapy to cure their disease. Some doctors focused on the most obvious symptoms, prescribing extra vitamins and minerals to counteract the emaciation cancer caused. Others recommended starvation diets for their patients in an effort to prevent the cancer from spreading by depriving it of nutrients. Some theories indicated that cancers were caused by unidentified organisms that infect healthy tissue; people went as far as to inject their tumors with extracts from animal parts such as spleens, bone marrow, lymph nodes, pancreas, stomach, and small intestine, hoping that something in the extracts could kill the cancer-causing organisms.

Not until the end of the nineteenth century did another form of cancer treatment become available. In 1895, a German professor named Wilhelm Conrad Roentgen discovered the X-ray purely by accident. While investigating how far cathode rays can travel, Roentgen noticed a glowing screen on the other side of his laboratory. He examined the screen more closely and discovered that if his hand was placed between the cathode ray tube and the screen, he could clearly see an outline of the bones of his hand. The X-ray, as Roentgen named it, was soon being used for things like the diagnosis of fractures and kidney stones. Having learned the penetrating power of X-rays, doctors exposed their cancer patients to X-rays in the hope of a curative effect. Soon doctors were reporting that tumors deep within patients' bodies had been cured using X-rays.

The discovery of radium by Pierre and Marie Curie led to a similar advance in cancer treatment. The Curies were interested in finding new elements that have radioactive properties. At the time, uranium and thorium were the only elements known to be radioactive. After years of studying uranium-containing minerals, the Curies were able to isolate radium, an element that is 2 million times more radioactive than uranium. Marie Curie writes: "The most important property of the rays is the production of physiological effects on the cells of the human organism. These effects may be used for the cure of several diseases. . . . What is considered particularly important is the treatment of cancer."[3] In the hope of effecting cures, doctors began placing small fragments of radium in contact with patients' tumors.

Radiation became a routine therapy for cancer within three years of Roentgen's initial discovery. Soon, however, it became clear that radiation could be harmful as well. Otherwise healthy people who worked with radiation began developing cancer. Whatever it was that radiation therapy was doing that killed cancer cells also was affecting normal cells in negative ways. Radiation, then, could treat cancer, but it could also cause cancer. It seemed that some other form of treatment would have to be found.

A Novel Idea

In fact, the early steps that would lead to chemical therapies for cancer had already been taken. The first of these advances was the gaining of a new insight into the nature of cells, the building blocks from which all living organisms are constructed. In the 1800s, the theory of spontaneous generation (the appearance of living organisms where none had previously existed) was widely accepted even by scientists. This view extended to disease; it was widely held that diseases like cancer merely arose under certain conditions.

In 1860, a German pathologist named Rudolf Virchow changed this view of the world with his theory that cells arise from other cells: "Where a cell arises, there a cell must have previously existed . . . just as an animal can spring only from an animal, a plant from a plant."[4] Virchow's insight also suggested that diseased cells arise from other diseased cells; as a result, for the first time, scientists began to seriously consider the role of the cell in cancer.

Virchow's work led other scientists to examine what differences, if any, there were between cancerous and noncancerous cells. It was already known that tumor cells grew faster than other cells, and it was soon discovered that cancer cells looked different from healthy cells under a microscope. Now, microscopic examination could help confirm the success of a surgical procedure. If the tissue removed by the surgeon consisted only of tumor cells, there was a good chance that the tumor had not been removed in its entirety; on the

Under a microscope, cancer cells (number 2) look strikingly different from their healthy counterparts (numbers 1 and 3).

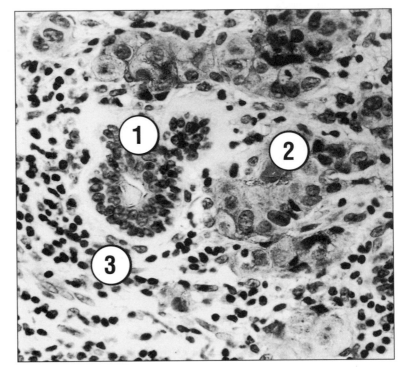

other hand, if healthy cells were detected on the periphery of the excised tissue, it was more likely that the tumor removal was complete.

The Man with Many-Colored Fingers

Microscopic examination could not explain exactly what made cancer cells look different, but given that there was a difference between cancerous and normal cells, the idea of using chemicals to target these diseased cells began to make sense. One of the first people to think about ways to use chemicals to target disease was German scientist Paul Ehrlich. From early in his career, Ehrlich was fascinated both with the cells of the human body and with chemical dyes. He noticed that some dyes stained certain cells while others did not. Sometimes a dye would stain a part of a cell in one type of tissue and have absolutely no effect on other tissues. For example, Ehrlich was the first to notice that a dye called methylene blue stained nerve endings—

and only nerve endings—when injected into live rats. Ehrlich's interest in why and how specific chemicals reacted with particular cell types would last a lifetime.

Ehrlich spent so much time experimenting with dyes that his medical school classmates from the Charité Hospital in Berlin remembered him as the man with red, blue, and green fingers. Ehrlich took any tissue sample he could get his hands on and tried to stain it with a variety of chemical dyes.

Ehrlich's work led him to form a theory that said there could be a chemical cure for every disease. He theorized that if certain dyes would only stain certain cells, other sorts of chemicals could specifically target the various single-cell microbes that caused so many illnesses in humans. He thought that by understanding the specific affinities of cells for different chemicals, scientists could design drugs to target diseases. Chemicals, Ehrlich suggested, could cure disorders by killing harmful cells without damaging vital tissues in the patient's body.

The Magic Bullet

In 1906, Ehrlich made a prophecy with regard to the way illness would be treated:

> If we picture an organism as infected by a certain species of bacterium, it will . . . be easy to effect a cure if substances have been discovered which have a specific affinity for these bacteria and act . . . on these alone . . . while possessing no affinity whatever for the normal constituents of the body, and cannot . . . have the least harmful . . . effect on the body. Such substances would then be . . . magic bullets which seek their target of their own accord.[5]

Ehrlich's search for magic bullets represented the first step toward modern day chemotherapy.

His colleagues, however, dismissed Ehrlich's ideas as far-fetched. They dubbed him Dr. Fantasy and laughed at him behind his back. Yet Ehrlich remained stubbornly convinced that he was right. He continued to search for chemicals that could combat disease at the cellular level. That search involved not a cure for cancer but a cure for a far more troublesome malady in some parts of the world: African trypanosomiasis, or sleeping sickness.

Ehrlich knew that the tsetse fly transmitted sleeping sickness. He also knew that a person with sleeping sickness suffered from fever, lethargy, and pain that ultimately ended in coma and death. Very real political pressures were driving researchers to come up with a treatment for this disease. At the time, Europeans were anxious to establish colonies in Africa, where sleeping sickness was endemic. Germany stood to gain access to valuable resources if it could colonize Africa before rival nations could; keeping colonists—and the natives they hoped would supply the needed labor—healthy was seen as the key to that effort.

Scientists knew that microorganisms called trypanosomes caused sleeping sickness. Ehrlich wanted to find a magic bullet that could kill these trypanosomes. Almost immediately, he found a dye, trypan red, that when injected into mice infected with trypanosomes cured them. Yet for all the good trypan red did in mice, Ehrlich learned that for some reason trypan red did not work effectively in human patients.

Ehrlich did not give up. Instead, he tried another approach to cure sleeping sickness. In 1899, an Englishman named H.W. Thomas had found that an arsenic-based compound, atoxyl, was effective in killing trypanosomes. Arsenic had been used since ancient times to treat various ailments. Thomas discovered that atoxyl helped cure some human patients of sleeping sickness, but it had one nasty side effect— it was not uncommon for the patient to go blind after taking the drug. Ehrlich believed that atoxyl could be the starting point in the effort to find the magic bullet for sleeping sickness. He decided to modify atoxyl, creating chemical compounds similar to the original drug but which did not cause such severe problems.

German scientist Paul Ehrlich first theorized that chemicals could be used to combat disease at the cellular level.

Over the next three years, Ehrlich tested more than six hundred different compounds. Some of the chemicals caused a fatal jaundice in the lab mice; others caused a strange change in their behavior that led them to jump and dance frantically until they died. Only two compounds seemed of any value—but not for sleeping sickness. Compounds 418 and 606 showed promise against spirochetes, the microorganisms that caused the sexually transmitted disease syphilis. They showed so much promise, in fact, that Ehrlich abandoned the search for other sleeping sickness treatments and focused only on killing spirochetes.

The Birth of Chemotherapy

In the end, it was compound 606 that was most effective against spirochetes. This compound's tongue-twisting name was dihydroxydiaminoarsenoben-zenedihydrochloride, but Ehrlich called it Salvarsan. Literally, the word *Salvarsan* means "that which saves with arsenic." Indeed, it cured rabbits of all symptoms of syphilis in lab tests. When Ehrlich tested Salvarsan on patients with syphilis, he found that many of those patients fully recovered. Later, in a clinical trial conducted in the Russian city of St. Petersburg, fifty-one out of fifty-five syphilis patients treated with Salvarsan made a complete recovery. Ehrlich called this method of treatment—curing disease with chemicals—chemotherapy.

Salvarsan proved to be an enormously important advance in treating an ancient scourge, but it had one drawback. If Salvarsan was accidentally injected into muscle or other tissue instead of a vein, the tissue was so severely damaged that the affected limb often had to be amputated. In response, Ehrlich developed a similar compound called Neosalvarsan, the new Salvarsan. Neosalvarsan was not as powerful in killing spirochetes as Salvarsan, but it was far safer to administer. These two drugs became part of the standard treatment for syphilis.

Ehrlich's ideas about magic bullets were the basis for the modern science of cancer chemotherapy. His work guided the research of other scientists as they searched for the magic bullet to cure cancer. Within a century, Ehrlich's concept of the magic bullet would change the world and the lives of cancer patients dramatically.

CHAPTER 2

Poisons That Heal

As the early work in developing cures for sleeping sickness and syphilis suggested, compounds that were potentially harmful, if carefully used, could be therapeutic. Indeed, the first drug that showed the potential to fight cancer was a poison called mustard gas, which had been used in World War I by the Germans against Allied troops.

Chemicals and Cancer

Even before scientists began studying the use of poisons to treat cancer, they were interested in how certain chemicals known as carcinogens could cause cancer. In 1775 an English surgeon named Sir Percival Plott conducted the first systematic study of cancer in London's chimney sweeps. Boys as young as seven years old were often employed as chimney sweeps because they were small enough to climb into narrow chimneys to scrape sooty residues off the inner walls. Plott noticed that, despite their youth, these chimney sweeps developed cancer at a higher rate than most people. Since cancer was known to be most common in the elderly, Plott found these cases of cancer worthy of careful study.

Chimney sweeping was a dirty job, and Plott noticed that the soot with which chimney sweeps were perpetually covered was the biggest difference between them and everyone else. While most people rarely had contact with chimney soot, the sweeps lived and breathed this residue, which contained a cancer-causing agent called coal tar. Eventually, Plott was able to link the frequency of cancer in chimney sweeps to their exposure to coal tar in the chimneys. This study was one of the first to distinguish a scientific link between a chemical and its ability to cause cancer. The use of chemicals to cure cancer, however, was still over a century away.

Scientists purify mustard gas during World War II. Mustard gas was the first poison to show promise as a cancer treatment.

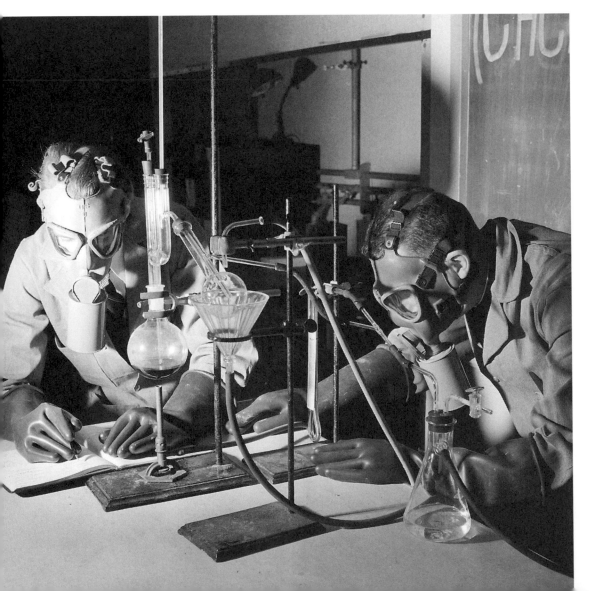

A Deadly Weapon

As it turned out, the first chemical to show promise in treating cancer was, paradoxically, known to cause cancer. During World War I, the Germans developed mustard gas as a chemical warfare agent. Mustard gas was a very powerful weapon because it caused skin blisters, damage to the respiratory tract and eyes, and substantial internal injuries. People exposed to mustard gas were typically left with dramatically reduced numbers of white blood cells and injury to their bone marrow. As a result, if the mustard gas failed to kill the victim immediately, it often caused serious health problems that would eventually prove fatal.

After German forces fired artillery shells loaded with mustard gas at Allied troops, Allied forces also began enhancing their weapons with mustard gas. For example, the American military added mustard gas to bombs to make them more lethal. The military was interested in documenting the effects of mustard gas as an offensive weapon. It also wanted to understand the consequences American troops would suffer after being exposed to this poison. To this end, a number of scientists in the United States studied mustard gas.

The first scientist to describe the medical effects of mustard gas was Edward Krumbhaar, who published his results in 1919. Krumbhaar noticed that a patient with mustard gas poisoning was most likely to die within two weeks of the exposure. By that time, many of the patient's bone marrow cells had been destroyed, and the patient was likely to develop pneumonia as a result of leucopenia (a reduction in the total number of white blood cells circulating in the body). Autopsies of mustard gas victims revealed extensive damage to many types of tissues; often the patient's bone marrow had lost its ability to regenerate.

The fact that many of those people whom mustard gas failed to kill outright eventually developed cancer was of interest to cancer researchers. This observation was tested experimentally in lab animals. Scientists found that just as in humans, as little as a single exposure to mustard gas could cause tumors to form in lab mice. Experiment after experiment seemed to indicate that mustard gas was a powerful carcinogen. This led other scientists, both within and outside the American military, to begin their own research into mustard gas and its cancer-causing properties.

A Novel Use for Poison

At the time that Krumbhaar was studying mustard gas, another researcher, Isaac Berenblum, began experiments to study the carcinogenic properties of many different chemicals. His studies included revisiting the carcinogenic properties of coal tar as well as studying the effects of mustard gas on tumor growth.

At first, Berenblum studied skin lesions in mice caused by coal tar—the same chemical Plott had identified in the late 1700s. By then, scientists had established that coal tar contains benzo(a)pyrene, one of the most potent carcinogens known. Yet, by itself, coal tar could not make tumors grow. Berenblum realized that other chemicals had to be applied to cause tumor growth.

Since research from World War I showed that mustard gas was carcinogenic, Berenblum decided to use it in his studies. In an experiment in 1929, he tried to speed up the growth of a coal tar tumor by adding some mustard gas to the skin of a mouse. Berenblum assumed that a small amount of carcinogenic mustard gas would make it easier for the tumor to grow, but surprisingly, the exact opposite happened. The small dose of mustard gas actually reduced the size of the tumor. Next, Berenblum applied small amounts of mustard gas to tumors caused by other carcinogens, and those tumors shrank as well. Eventually, he realized that in low enough doses, mustard gas might actually benefit cancer patients by causing their tumors to shrink or even disappear altogether.

Still, mustard gas was a powerful poison and so was of limited use. Scientists remembered how Paul Ehrlich had altered arsenic compounds to cure syphilis and later was able to alter them further to reduce unwanted side effects. They began to wonder if mustard gases could be modified to treat cancer without the adverse side effects that made it an effective weapon.

The Wartime Effort

During World War II, Berenblum's conclusions about the implications of mustard gas for cancer therapy

The John Harvey, *an Allied cargo ship sunk during the German air raid over Bari, released huge amounts of mustard gas into the air. Over six hundred soldiers were exposed to the poison.*

were corroborated by the accidental exposure of American and other Allied troops. On December 2, 1943, about fifty Allied ships crowded the harbor in the Italian port of Bari. Unexpectedly, German bombers attacked the harbor and within twenty minutes, the worst bombing of an Allied port since Pearl Harbor two years earlier was over. Sixteen ships were sunk, four were partially destroyed, and hundreds of men were injured.

Such a disaster would have been devastating under any circumstances, but among the Allied ships that were sunk was the *S.S. John Harvey*, which was carrying a top-secret cargo of two thousand bombs loaded with mustard gas. During the attack, the *John Harvey* was destroyed, and its deadly cargo was released into the air and into the ocean. The poison gas alarm was sounded, but only belatedly, and even then people on the scene did not know what chemical was involved. By the time gas masks were issued, more than six hundred Allied soldiers had already been exposed to mustard gas.

As fires spread in the stricken vessels, men jumped into the water to escape their burning ships. Unknowingly, they dove into a poisonous sea of mustard gas. They suffered horrible chemical burns, blindness, and internal damage from swallowing the poisoned water. Still others unwittingly inhaled poisonous fumes from the burning cargo as they battled the flames in the harbor.

One witness to the catastrophe was U.S. Army colonel Cornelius Packard Rhoads, who was also a doctor. In the aftermath, Rhoads, who at the time did not know about the *John Harvey*'s cargo, treated many of the survivors. Although the military did not disclose the nature of the poison carried by the *John Harvey*, Rhoads knew that the survivors must have been exposed to some kind of chemical agent—the types of injuries he was treating most frequently were only consistent with chemical weapons exposure.

The Structure of DNA

In 1953 James Watson and Francis Crick discovered the structure of DNA, which opened the doors to a greater understanding of human biology at a molecular level. The structure they revealed was, in many ways, extremely simple—a molecule of DNA consists of two strands, with each strand being a series of sugars, phosphates, and nucleotide bases.

There are four different nucleotide bases found in DNA: adenine, cytosine, guanine, and thymine. The two strands of DNA are paired at the level of the nucleotide bases. An adenine on one strand will only pair with a thymine on the other; similarly, guanine will pair only with cytosine. It is the pairing of the nucleotide bases that keeps the double-stranded DNA molecule zipped together.

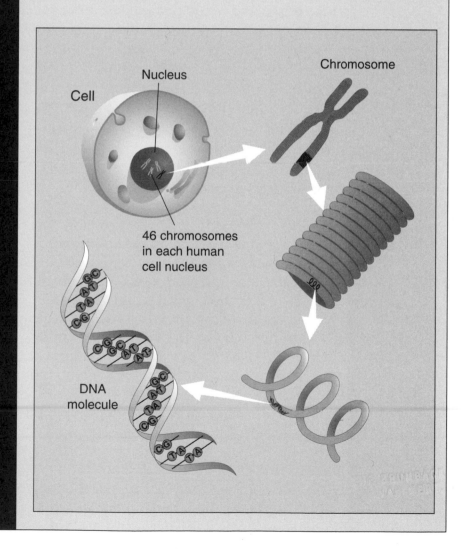

In the days following the bombing, Rhoads noticed that the survivors experienced significant changes in their white blood cell counts. He writes: "These casualties showed at first a moderate elevation of white blood count . . . followed on about the second day by a profound drop or total disappearance of [white blood cells]."[6] Eventually, the military disclosed that the chemical involved was mustard gas. Rhoads, who was familiar with Berenblum's work with mustard gas, formed a theory about the chemical and its potential to fight some kinds of cancer. He reasoned that if the chemical ingredients of mustard gas were responsible for the reduction of white blood cells, they might be useful against certain types of leukemia, a form of cancer in which the body produces too many white blood cells. Rhoads knew that mustard gas itself could not be used because of the severe side effects it caused, such as damage to the patient's bone marrow. Instead, he proposed that chemicals similar to mustard gas be tested as anticancer drugs.

A Subtle Change

At the same time that Rhoads was forming his ideas about the use of mustard gas, scientists back home in the United States arrived at the same conclusions about using this chemical as a starting point for anticancer drugs. The mustard gases used in Berenblum's early experiments and in the warheads in Bari were sulfur-based compounds, so the first approach scientists took was to alter the sulfur content of mustard gas. When the sulfur atoms were replaced by nitrogen atoms, a new class of compounds, called nitrogen mustards, was created.

Since the military had an interest in further research into mustard gas and related compounds, the military's Office of Scientific Research and Development signed a contract with Yale University to investigate these chemical warfare agents. In 1942 a large team of scientists, led by Alfred Gilman, Louis Goodman, and Fred Philips, was assigned by Yale and the army to explore nitrogen mustards as possible chemotherapy drugs. At first, Gilman, Goodman, and Philips tested nitrogen mustards on lab mice. They teamed up with an anatomist named Thomas Dougherty to figure out how much nitrogen mustard an animal could tolerate before dying and how the side effects of nitrogen mustard on bone marrow correlated to the amount of drug administered.

These researchers treated the tumor of a laboratory mouse with injections of nitrogen mustard. After two injections, the tumor started to shrink until it was no longer detectable by touch. After the initial course of nitrogen mustard was stopped, the tumor reappeared. The scientists successfully treated the mouse a second time with another set of nitrogen mustard injections. From past experiments, they knew that mice with this particular type of tumor usually lived about three weeks. With the nitrogen mustard therapy, this mouse lived for eighty-four days.

From Mouse to Man

In the same hospital at Yale where the animal tests of nitrogen mustards were being conducted, human cancer patients were also being treated. One of the doctors, an assistant professor of surgery named Gustaf Lindskog, was seriously concerned about one of his patients, a forty-eight-year-old man with non-Hodgkin's lymphoma. The patient's cancer had already spread, and at the time, radiation therapy was the only available treatment for metastasized cancers. The man, known as J.D., had already suffered through numerous rounds of radiation therapy. Unfortunately for J.D., his cancer was not responding to the radiation and was getting worse.

Lymphomas are cancers that affect the lymphatic system. The lymphatic system is a specialized component

Until chemotherapy drugs were developed in the 1960s, radiation therapy was the most effective cancer treatment.

of the circulatory system that carries lymphatic fluid through the body. Among other functions, this fluid plays a key role in the immune system's response to diseases in that it contains disease-fighting white blood cells. In non-Hodgkin's lymphoma, the number of white blood cells known as B cells and T cells in the lymphatic fluid increase to dangerous and cancerous levels. When the body loses control over the growth of these cells, they overcrowd the tissues of the lymph glands and eventually destroy them. As this cancer advances, it can destroy other organs as well.

Based on the positive results of the trial of nitrogen mustards on the laboratory mouse, Gilman and the rest of his team thought J.D. would be an ideal candidate for nitrogen mustard therapy. The research team knew from the previous animal experiments that lymphoid tissue was especially sensitive to nitrogen mustards; therefore, they believed a lymphoma might be treatable with this type of chemical. Furthermore, nothing else was working, and J.D. was facing certain death from his cancer. Gilman persuaded Lindskog to begin clinical trials of nitrogen mustards with J.D. as the first patient.

Over the next ten days, J.D. received one hundred doses of nitrogen mustard intravenously. Within forty-eight hours, his tumors had begun to soften. By the fourth day of therapy, his doctors noticed that many of the tumors were no longer detectable by touch. By the end of the ten days, Gilman and Goodman wrote, "All signs and symptoms due to the disease disappeared."[7]

The improvements proved to be temporary, and unfortunately, J.D. suffered damage to his bone marrow. This side effect prevented his doctors from trying more nitrogen mustard therapy, and eventually J.D. died of complications from his cancer. The results were extremely encouraging, however, and other medical professionals received them with enthusiasm. Rhoads, whose own interest in chemotherapy had continued, later wrote of this case: "A new fact had been established. . . . A chemical compound was at hand which would [adversely] affect [cancers] reputedly resistant to x-rays."[8]

Further clinical trials were conducted based on the positive initial results Lindskog saw. Nitrogen mustard therapy was tried next on a thirty-three-year-old woman, known as L.W., who had Hodgkin's disease, another type of lymphoma. This patient received four doses of nitrogen mustard, and a number of improvements were reported. Before the treatment, L.W.'s face had become swollen and distorted, and she had enlarged masses in her neck, arms, and chest. After treatment, the swelling in L.W.'s face was greatly diminished and she no longer appeared disfigured.

Alkylating Agents

The class of drugs derived from nitrogen mustards are called alkylating agents because of the specific chemical reaction that these drugs cause when they interact with the DNA of a cell. Normally, DNA is a molecule made up of two long strands of bases zipped together. When an alkylating agent comes in contact with a molecule of DNA, it interferes with the DNA zipper. These chemicals hang a molecular fragment on the bases of the strand of DNA. Once the molecular fragment is attached to a DNA base, it can no longer pair up with the other strand correctly. This chemical modification makes the zipper unravel. Molecules of DNA treated with alkylating agents are more prone to breakage or other problems that can lead to the death of the cell.

The other hard masses softened considerably as well. According to her doctors, "The dramatic therapeutic remission persisted until it was interrupted at the end of four weeks by [other medical circumstances that prevented further treatment]."[9]

Overall, thirteen patients with non-Hodgkin's lymphoma and twenty-seven patients with Hodgkin's disease were treated with nitrogen mustard in the initial clinical trial. "In nearly every case [of Hodgkin's disease] some benefit was obtained from chemotherapy. . . . In addition to rapid partial or complete disappearance of Hodgkin's tumor masses, most patients experienced improvement in appetite, weight, strength, and sense of well-being,"[10] write Gilman and Goodman. Most of the non-Hodgkin's lymphoma patients also showed great improvement, but for unknown reasons, the therapy sometimes did not work. "At least five complete failures were encountered without obvious explanation for the lack of satisfactory response,"[11] notes Goodman. Nevertheless, when the nitrogen mustard was effective, even patients on the brink of death showed dramatic improvement.

A Stroke of Luck

The drugs that were eventually developed as a result of all the work on nitrogen mustards shared structural similarities with mustard gas, but scientists had made enough substitutions in the structure to eliminate most of the deadly side effects of the original chemical. By the 1960s, new drugs like mechlorethamine, cyclophosphamide, chlorambucil, and melphalan were being used to treat a range of blood cancers, including lymphomas and leukemias. These compounds made up a new class of drugs known as alkylating agents. The name alkylating agent refers to the fact that these drugs chemically modify a cell's DNA by attaching a chemical structure known as an alkyl group.

The new alkylating agents represented a dramatic step forward in treating some cancers, yet they were by no means a universal cancer cure. Just as there were failures reported in treating non-Hodgkin's lymphoma and Hodgkin's disease, the Yale research team's later tests of nitrogen mustards on other types of cancers, such as melanoma, cervical carcinoma, and even other lymphomas, in both humans and animals, did not show the same dramatic levels of success. Indeed, it was only by a stroke of luck that the researchers chose to study the effect of nitrogen mustards on exactly the types of cancer against which they were most effective. Gilman later wrote, "I have often thought that if we had by accident chosen one of these [cancers] in which there was absolutely no therapeutic effect, we might possibly have dropped the whole project."[12] Without this good fortune, chemotherapy would not have received its first nod of approval.

The conclusions that Gilman, Goodman, and Philips drew from their clinical trials had the medical field buzzing with excitement. The fact that the nitrogen mustards were not a long-lasting cure for cancer was irrelevant. According to Gilman biographer Murdoch Ritchie: "The point is that tumor growth had been clearly shown to be susceptible to chemotherapy, and treatment was no longer limited just to radiation or to radical surgery. From this insightful beginning medical oncology grew and now is one of the recognized medical subspecialties."[13] For the first time, a magic bullet for cancer seemed a real possibility.

CHAPTER 3

The Early Arsenal

The alkylating agents that worked against certain cancers were valuable tools, but the new drugs could not treat all the different types of cancer that affected humans; in fact, early clinical trials showed that even patients with the same type of cancer would not all respond well to the drugs they were given. Still, in the 1940s, heartened by their early success, scientists began reexamining older herbal treatments and breaking new ground by synthesizing new chemicals based on modern principles. The goal was to examine every possible solution, and the fruits of these scientists' labor proved to be priceless.

Vitamin Therapy

While Gilman, Goodman, and Philips focused on altering poisons to fight cancer, other scientists took a variety of different approaches. One of these scientists was Sidney Farber, who was a pathologist at Children's Hospital in Boston in the mid-1940s. Farber thought an essential vitamin—folic acid—might hold the key to curing leukemia.

In his line of work, Farber saw many children suffering from leukemia, and he felt a personal responsibility to find a cure. In the beginning, however, the best Farber could do was treat his patients' symptoms. One of the symptoms that Farber commonly dealt with was anemia.

Anemia is a condition in which too few red blood cells, which carry oxygen throughout the body, are produced, resulting in fatigue and weakness. The usual treatment for most types of anemia had been to administer very large doses of folic acid. Farber, however,

A Disease of Immortality

Normal, healthy cells wait for a signal from the body to divide. Cancer cells, on the other hand, are stuck on fast-forward—their division is rapid and unregulated, which leads to a large increase in the number of cancerous cells. This explains why tumors grow faster than other types of tissues. This problem with cell division is what makes cancer so difficult to fight. When cancerous cells divide uncontrollably, they take over the body's resources to feed their own ravenous appetites. The body is forced to wage war on itself to keep the cancer at bay.

Through various genetic mutations, cancer grants immortality to diseased cells. This ultimately results in an unsustainable increase in the number of cancer cells and the death of its victim. The body ordinarily regulates the number of cells of a certain type by controlling the rate of cell division and the rate of cell death. Every cell in the body is equipped with a detection system to constantly monitor whether there are too many cells of that type in an area or whether it has become unhealthy. If conditions arise where a cell's death would be more beneficial to the body than its continued life, it will initiate a process of events to end its life. In essence, cells are programmed to commit suicide when ordered

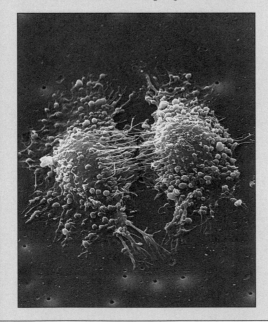

to do so by the body. In this way, cells do not multiply inappropriately, and sick cells do not reproduce to create more unhealthy cells. Cancer cells lack these controls, and therefore do not die on their own; in a sense, they are immortal—it takes an outside influence to kill them.

Without some form of treatment, cancer cells like this one divide rapidly and uncontrollably.

noticed that this treatment seemed to cause his leukemia patients' cancers to progress at an accelerated rate. In fact, the number of white blood cells in patients treated with folic acid suddenly skyrocketed. Farber concluded that folic acid could somehow stimulate the growth and maturation of all types of bone marrow cells. If additional folic acid produced more blood cells, he reasoned, a chemical that blocked the action of folic acid might reduce the number of blood cells made, and perhaps this blocking agent, or antagonist, could be used to treat leukemia.

These observations inspired the chemists at a pharmaceutical company called Lederle to synthesize new folic acid antagonists. Eventually, they developed aminopterin. Aminopterin is a chemical that is very similar in structure to folic acid. Where folic acid was a usable chemical inside a cell, however, aminopterin acted like a monkey wrench. A cell would take in aminopterin in the same way it would normally take in folic acid, but instead of stimulating cell growth, the drug would counteract the effects of folic acid and cause the cell to die. In 1947, Farber administered aminopterin to sixteen children with leukemia. Ten of those children went into remission (a state in which the symptoms of cancer are significantly reduced or disappear altogether even though cancer cells may still be present in the body); one of them went for forty-three days without additional chemotherapy.

Farber's work marked the beginning of the successful use of a new class of drugs to treat cancer. These drugs were called antimetabolites, because they interfered with the normal metabolism of a cell. As cancer cells were known to grow and divide faster than normal cells, drugs that killed cells by interfering with metabolism were particularly effective against cancer.

Further Progress

Based on Farber's successes, scientists agreed that aminopterin seemed very promising as a leukemia treatment. It did have drawbacks, however. Farber knew, for example, that among aminopterin's many negative side effects was that it was very toxic to other parts of a patient's body. When aminopterin was administered, the resulting deficiency in folic acid affected normal cells as well as cancer cells; this deficiency often resulted in an increased risk of vascular disease and cognitive disorders. Also, the remissions from aminopterin treatment seemed to be temporary. Farber and his colleagues at Lederle continued to search for a more effective leukemia drug. Following the example of Ehrlich, they altered the existing drug and tested the new substances for efficacy against cancer. Two years after he tested aminopterin, Farber developed another drug, methotrexate.

Methotrexate, although still a folic acid antagonist, presented fewer side effects than aminopterin. Patients treated with methotrexate suffer damage to normal tissue that is similar to the damage caused by aminopterin, but often to a less severe degree. Although the remissions were initially temporary, as with aminopterin, methotrexate enjoyed greater success than its predecessor because of its milder side effects. Another plus was that the side effects of methotrexate can be mitigated because this drug has an antidote of sorts. The antidrug known as leukovorin can halt the negative effects of methotrexate.

Rescue and Recognition

Leukovorin was a drug form of folic acid, developed in 1964 by Isaac Djerassi. While working with Farber, Djerassi realized that the low doses in which methotrexate was being administered resulted in low side effects but somewhat ineffective action against cancer. A higher dose, he realized, would be much more successful in stopping cancer cells from spreading, but this level of medication would not be safe for the patient. He concluded that an antidote was needed to counter the harmful effects of methotrexate after all the patient's

The Mystery of Jimmy

In order to treat the large number of patients at Boston's Children's Hospital, pathologist Sidney Farber's job included raising money for research. To that end, in 1948, there was a radio fund-raiser. Members of the Boston Braves appeared on the broadcast, along with an anonymous 12-year-old boy suffering from cancer who led the singing of "Take Me Out to the Ballgame." Farber insisted that the press respect the boy's privacy but was pressed for a name. In Dan Shaughnessy's *Boston Globe* article, "A Mystery Story With a Happy Ending: Even Dana-Farber Was Left Clueless," which ran on May 17, 1998, Farber's naming of the Jimmy Fund was spontaneous. As he said: "I said, in desperation, 'Well, call him Jimmy!' And that's how the title came about."

The Jimmy Fund became a very successful charity enterprise, patronized by such celebrities as baseball great Ted Williams. But over the years the true identity of Jimmy remained a mystery. When Farber died in 1973, even the administrators at Children's Hospital thought Jimmy's real name was lost forever.

During that time, many stories sprang up about the real Jimmy. Some

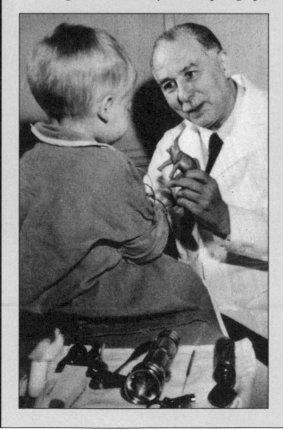

claimed he died five months after the radio broadcast, that he was named Steven, or that he lived on Long Island. Finally, in 1997, Jimmy Fund director Mike Andrews received a letter from a woman claiming to be the real Jimmy's sister. Ten months later, the mystery was solved: Jimmy was actually Carl Einar Gustafson, a boy who was cured by Farber's chemotherapy regimen.

Dr. Sidney Farber launched the Jimmy Fund in 1948 to raise money for cancer research.

cancer cells had been destroyed. This antidote was called leukovorin. By properly timing the administration of methotrexate and leukovorin, cancer cells could be treated without seriously damaging the rest of the body.

The process of administering leukovorin directly following methotrexate was called rescue, since the patients were rescued by the antidote from harmful side effects of the cancer treatment. With the development of a rescue drug, the effects of methotrexate could be modified at will. Farber, Djerassi, and their collaborators recognized this benefit, and began using high dose methotrexate therapy in combination with rescue to treat and cure many virulent childhood cancers.

George Hitchings and Gertrude Elion proved that artificial purines, key components of cellular DNA, could be used to kill cancer cells.

Another advantage of using folic acid antagonists was that they did not specifically act against a particular type of cancer cell. In 1956, the first case of metastatic cancer was cured using methotrexate. Roy Hertz and Min Chiu Li successfully treated patients suffering from choriocarcinoma, a cancer of the placenta, with a three- to five-day course of methotrexate followed by an antibiotic called actinomycin-D. Other success stories soon followed.

Just like the scientists who worked with alkylating agents, neither Farber nor his contemporaries fully understood the mechanism by which these new chemotherapy drugs were able to treat cancer. It was known that the drugs interfered with cell division, but it was still unclear what part of the process was disrupted or even whether the different drugs acted on different cellular targets. Nevertheless, Farber understood that it was unnecessary, as he said, to have "the full solution of all the problems of basic research. . . . The history of medicine is replete with examples of cures obtained years, decades, and even centuries before the mechanism of action was understood."[14] Despite this lack of understanding the mechanisms of the drugs' actions, chemotherapy was gradually changing the way cancer was fought.

A Rational Approach

Farber was not the only person hoping to treat cancer with drugs that block a cell's metabolism and interfere with its reproduction. In 1942 a pharmaceutical company called Wellcome Research Laboratories hired a researcher named George Hitchings to head up the biochemistry department. Although he was the head as well as the only member of the department, Hitchings accepted the position because he saw one great advantage: "I was free to develop my own program of research."[15]

In 1944 Hitchings hired another scientist, Gertrude Elion, to assist him. They focused their attention on compounds that resembled purines, which they knew were key components of a cell's genetic material, DNA. If they could make a compound that cells could not distinguish from normal purines, that compound could interfere with DNA replication and thereby block cell division. The principle was similar to Farber's use of folic acid antagonists. Elion later recalled that she and Hitchings speculated that "since all cells required nucleic acids, it might be possible to stop the growth of rapidly dividing cells [like cancer cells] with antagonists of the nucleic acid bases."[16]

This was a somewhat risky approach, as Hitchings and Elion did not conclusively know that artificial purines would interfere with cell division. Elion later said, "[We] didn't know the structure of DNA, because nobody did at the time, but [we] knew what the building blocks were, and so we were starting really at the very basic portion of the DNA and saying we don't know how it gets to be DNA . . . but let's find out how we can deal with it."[17]

By 1949, Hitchings and Elion had synthesized a new compound called diaminopurine that looked promising as a treatment for cancer. The two scientists had shown that diaminopurine was able to inhibit the growth of cancerous cells in mice. A doctor named Joseph Burchenal at Sloan-Kettering Institute tested diaminopurine in four patients with leukemia. He found that two of them went into remission. But the side effects of diaminopurine were unbearable to most patients—the nausea and vomiting this drug caused were so severe, malnutrition would result if therapy continued for too long.

Diaminopurine was disappointing to its developers in that it did not cure leukemia, but it was not a complete failure. Even if the side effects of the drug prevented it from becoming a widely used treatment, Hitchings and Elion had proven that an artificial purine did kill cancer cells. Now they concentrated on developing another similar purine-related compound, which they called 6-mercaptopurine, or 6-MP.

This new drug worked against leukemia without the harsh side effects of its predecessor. In fact, 6-MP generated so much excitement in the medical field that the U.S. Food and Drug Administration approved the drug for use in cancer patients just ten months after clinical trials began—an extremely short approval time. 6-MP in combination with other drugs became part of the standard treatment for childhood leukemia.

Healthy Hormones

The antimetabolite drugs that Farber, Hitchings, and Elion studied comprised only one of the new frontiers in chemotherapy research in the 1940s and 1950s. Research progressed as scientists explored the properties of all sorts of chemicals. For example, Charles Benton Huggins was turning the body's own chemicals against cancer as he pioneered the field of hormone therapy.

Sensational Cures

Farber's success with treating cancer in children gained him considerable publicity. Even while the folic acid antagonist treatment was considered experimental, desperate parents brought their children to Boston in the hopes that Farber could perform a miracle where no other treatment was working.

One such child was Carl Einar Gustafson. When Carl was twelve, he started feeling cramps in his stomach. Doctors in the small town where Carl lived immediately guessed that he was seriously ill with some form of cancer, but there was little they could do. Carl was in pain, even after the doctors performed two surgeries to treat his symptoms. The doctors told Carl's parents that Carl had six weeks to live.

Still, one of Carl's doctors decided to send him to Children's Hospital to consult with Farber, who diagnosed Carl with non-Hodgkin's lymphoma. At the time, this type of cancer had a cure rate of only 20 percent. Although the odds were against him, Farber agreed to treat Carl with surgery and his folic acid antagonist. Carl was to become one of the success stories. It took over a decade of regular trips to Boston for checkups and chemotherapy, but Carl was cured. He grew to be six foot five inches tall and married his high school sweetheart. Carl lived to age 65, when he succumbed not to cancer, but to a stroke.

In his search for an effective treatment of prostate cancer, Charles Huggins discovered that tumors respond to the female hormone estrogen.

The idea that, as Huggins said, "some types of cancer cells differ in a cardinal way from the cells from which they arose in their response to change in their hormonal environment"[18] was not actually new. A scientist named Thomas Beatson had come to the same conclusions almost half a century before. Beatson had noticed that rabbits whose ovaries had been removed stopped producing milk. In 1896, Beatson described his discoveries, saying, "This fact seemed to me of great interest, for it pointed to one organ holding control over the secretion of another and separate organ."[19] In this case, it was the ovaries holding control over the breasts. Beatson wondered if the ovaries might somehow also be involved in the development of breast cancer in humans. To test his hypothesis, Beatson removed the ovaries of two patients suffering from advanced breast cancer; he noticed improvements, such as tumor softening and shrinkage, in their cancer symptoms immediately. Beatson did not fully understand why removal of the ovaries helped breast cancer patients because hormones at that time were unknown. Huggins studied Beatson's work and used it as a guide, not to treat breast

cancer, but prostate cancer. Huggins and other scientists understood, as Beatson had not, that ovaries and testes produced sex hormones. Huggins realized that Beatson's experiments showed that hormones affected the growth of cancer cells, just as they did the growth of normal cells.

As a physician, Huggins treated many prostate cancer patients. He was among the first people to perform orchiectomies, or surgical castrations, on his prostate cancer patients. He noticed that castration, which served to eliminate a patient's sex hormones, greatly slowed the growth of tumors. This observation proved the existence of a type of cancer that was dependent on hormones for growth. Huggins later wrote: "The hormone-dependent cancer cell . . . grows in the presence of supporting hormones but it dies in their absence."[20] Huggins decided to refine the procedure for eliminating hormones: Instead of removing organs, he would try blocking the actions of the hormones those organs produced.

Huggins knew that regardless of gender, the human body makes both male and female sex hormones—men and women differ only in the proportions of each hormone that are made. Huggins believed that large doses of female sex hormones would have the same effect on prostate cancer as castration would, plus it would have the advantage of being a completely reversible treatment. Huggins injected the patients in his trial with the female hormone estrogen. He was reasonably sure that estrogen would be safe to use since men produce it anyway, albeit in small amounts.

The patients in Huggins' study were suffering from cancers that were inaccessible by surgery and did not respond to radiation. They had no alternatives left and had nothing to lose by trying the new treatment. The results of the estrogen therapy were extraordinary. In eighteen out of twenty-one cases, the patients' tumors shrank immediately and were prevented from spreading to other parts of the body. Huggins declared that

Robert Noble discovered that a chemical found in periwinkles could be used to fight leukemia.

"certain cancers are hormone-dependent and these cells die when supporting hormones are eliminated [or] when large amounts of [counteracting] hormones are administered."[21] This, in effect, created a new class of chemotherapy treatment based on hormones.

Getting Back to Nature

As interest in chemotherapy grew, virtually every class of chemicals drew the interest of researchers. It seemed as though the possibilities for chemotherapy were endless. For example, by exploiting the chemical properties of different compounds, researcher Hamao Umezawa developed the first anticancer antibiotic, phleomycin, and Barnett Rosenberg discovered cisplatin, the first in the class of inorganic chemotherapy drugs. Many of these drugs, which were developed in the early stages of chemotherapy, were similar in that they specifically acted on rapidly dividing populations of cells. The differences, however, lay in the types of cancers, and even types of patients, that could be treated with each drug.

As with the nitrogen mustard therapies, which were successful in some patients and showed no effect whatsoever in others, scientists soon found that the newer drugs were similarly unpredictable.

Because scientists could not determine, before development, the efficacy of a particular type of drug, research continued on multiple fronts. As important as synthesizing new compounds like methotrexate and 6-MP was, some researchers kept the value of naturally occurring substances in mind.

Robert Laing Noble was one of the scientists who placed a value on thousands of years of folk remedies for treating disease. In particular, he was interested in finding improved treatments for diabetes. Noble had learned that in Jamaica it was fairly common for people with diabetes to drink a tea made from periwinkle leaves when insulin was not available. Noble realized that identifying the compound in the periwinkle leaves that was effective against diabetes would be an important medical breakthrough.

After much research, Noble concluded that there was nothing specific in the periwinkle that made it useful against the symptoms of diabetes. He did, however, notice something unexpected: A reduction in white blood cells occurred in people who ingested periwinkle. Noble concluded that something in periwinkle could be useful against leukemia, which after all was caused by the overproduction of white blood cells. He began to search for the chemical responsible for this dramatic effect.

Noble started hunting for the active chemical agent in periwinkle leaves in 1954. It took four years of hard work by a team of scientists, including Noble. Eventually, they isolated a compound that Noble called vinblastine. It took another year to collect enough vinblastine to use in clinical trials. In the end, however, the search was fruitful—vinblastine proved very effective in the initial tests. Vinblastine and its chemically related cousins, the vinca alkaloids, suppress cell division by directly blocking the cellular machinery responsible for mitosis, or cell division. These medicines, called antimitotics, joined the growing arsenal of drugs to fight a variety of cancers.

A National Effort

Following up on Noble's efforts, the American government began to research naturally occurring chemotherapy drugs as well. In 1955, Congress established a National Chemotherapy Program as a part of the National Cancer Institute. Although the program did explore synthetic drugs, its largest focus was the start of a systematic approach to testing naturally occurring plants for potential therapeutic properties. In total, more than five hundred thousand chemicals from more than twelve thousand different species of plants were tested.

One of the biggest success stories of the National Chemotherapy Program was the 1962 discovery of a

Extracts from the Pacific yew tree are used to produce the drug Taxol, an effective treatment for breast and ovarian cancer.

special extract from the bark of a tree, the Pacific yew tree, *Taxus brevifolia*. This extract showed remarkable activity against a variety of tumors. The drug developed from this extract was named Taxol, and it rapidly became a common treatment for breast and ovarian cancers. Taxol, however, would be just one of forty-five new agents that were effective against twenty-nine forms of cancer, to be developed as a result of the National Chemotherapy Program in the next four decades.

In half a century, chemotherapy had gone from a theoretical possibility to a thriving science. The heart of traditional chemotherapy was established in six main classes: alkylating agents, antimetabolites, hormone therapies, antibiotics, inorganic drugs, and antimitotics. These six classes would comprise the core of traditional chemotherapy for decades, proving invaluable to thousands of cancer patients and saving countless lives. It was not, however, an unqualified success because all too often, chemotherapy drugs caused health problems of their own. The search for chemotherapy compounds that were also safe for patients to take would continue.

CHAPTER 4

The Problem with Poison

Every year, more than 1 million people in the United States alone receive chemotherapy. Although it helps hundreds of thousands of people survive cancer, most patients dread the thought of undergoing these treatments—not because they think they will not cure the cancer but because of the severity of the negative side effects. At the mere mention of the word chemotherapy, patients often envision themselves bald, exhausted, and vomiting, unable to concentrate and almost more sick from the chemotherapy than from the cancer.

On a basic level, chemotherapy is the very careful administration of poisons to kill cells. Most of the drugs used for chemotherapy are cytotoxic, meaning they have the potential to kill any cell. As one would expect, this poison sometimes goes out of control. Doctors can trace the causes of the most common side effects of chemotherapy directly to unintentional results of poison.

Near Death Experiences

As toxic as chemotherapy drugs can be, doctors usually manage to control the negative side effects by carefully controlling the doses. In fact, the drugs have the potential to be lethal if administered at very high levels. The problem, of course, is that the dose needed to kill off particularly troublesome tumors can be very close to the dose that will kill the patient.

The case of Dustin Fagan illustrates the problem. Dustin was only nine years old when a childhood brain cancer called medulloblastoma threatened to end his life. A cobwebby growth was slowly spreading through his brain, gradually colonizing the healthy areas and replacing them with cancer cells. Though doctors had administered treatments, nothing was stopping the cancer—not surgery, not radiation, not standard chemotherapy. The only option left to save Dustin's life was to nearly kill him.

Dustin's doctors planned to use the chemotherapy drug called cyclophosphamide at the highest possible levels to kill off every last cancer cell. Unfortunately, this plan would wipe out most of Dustin's gastrointestinal lining, his hair follicles, and almost all of his bone marrow cells as well. In addition, every part of Dustin's body would be damaged in some way by the

One of the most common side effects of chemotherapy is hair loss. Here, a chemotherapy patient who has lost her hair undergoes another round of treatment.

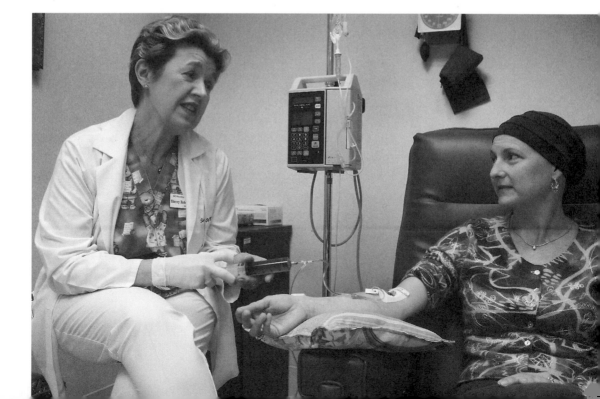

high doses this form of chemotherapy required. He would be able to eat only through a feeding tube; he would lose all his hair; and, most seriously, Dustin's immune system would be greatly compromised, leaving him open to life-threatening infections. Because of the damage to his immune system, he would need to have an autologous bone marrow transplant. This meant that, because the chemotherapy would destroy any bone marrow present in his body during treatment, some of his healthy bone marrow would be removed before the treatment, then injected back into Dustin's body after the treatment. Dustin suffered through almost every negative side effect of chemotherapy. In the end, however, he went on to live a normal, healthy life, free of cancer.

Treating the Body as a Whole

The problem Dustin's doctors, and any doctors administering chemotherapy, face is that it is for the most part a systemic treatment. This means the drugs travel throughout the body rather than being confined to the site of the cancer. Although some chemotherapy drugs can be injected directly into a tumor, the chemicals usually must enter the bloodstream in order to gain access to cancerous cells. This is especially true in the case of cancers that are not easily accessible, like Dustin's, as well as for cancer that has metastasized, or spread throughout the body.

Even in instances in which a cancer is relatively accessible and localized, chemotherapy is often administered intravenously. This is because chemotherapy administered intramuscularly (injected directly into a muscle) or subcutaneously (injected under the skin) can result in irritated or even damaged muscle or skin tissue due to the toxic nature of the drugs. A few chemotherapy drugs are available in the form of a pill to be taken orally, but this method has similar drawbacks: Just as muscle and skin can be damaged by chemotherapy drugs, the gastrointestinal lining is especially prone to irritation and injury.

In part, the problem with chemotherapy is the result of the nature of cancer itself. Unlike viruses and bacteria that invade the body, cancer cells look much like healthy cells to the human immune system. Whereas the body's own defenses are usually capable of beating invaders (although help from antibiotics or antiviral drugs is often needed), this does not hold true with cancer.

Cancer's Weak Point

The strategy against cancer is to attack its weak point, which is often its rapid growth rate. Drugs from each of the six main classes of chemotherapy all interfere with some aspect of cell division: they directly block the cellular machinery responsible for physically separating daughter cells, or they interfere with the cell's ability to replicate its DNA, or they damage the DNA so severely that it can no longer be replicated. Historically, scientists developed chemotherapy drugs that interfered with a cell's—any cell's—ability to divide. The rationale behind this was that since cancer cells had a faster growth rate than normal cells, at any given time, a higher proportion of cancer cells than normal cells would be in the process of cell division.

The problem, of course, is that just as the body's immune system cannot distinguish cancer cells from healthy ones, the chemotherapy drugs tend to kill both healthy and cancerous cells that are dividing. This is particularly true of cells that divide often, such as those in the blood, hair, and the lining of the stomach and intestines. When treated with traditional chemotherapy drugs, cancer patients were often left to cross their fingers and hope that all their cancer cells would be killed before too much healthy tissue died.

A Menu of Poisons

Because of the potentially severe side effects, doctors are careful to evaluate the benefits a particular course of chemotherapy offers the patient. Moreover, the side

Chemo Brain

Perhaps the most dreaded side effect of chemotherapy is a loss of cognitive function, often called chemo brain. Patients' concentration, memory, comprehension, and reasoning skills are affected. Some research indicates that chemo brain can persist up to ten years after treatment. Often this condition leaves cancer patients feeling more defeated by their disease, and depression commonly results.

Doctors are not sure what causes chemo brain and whether the cause lies in a certain amount or combination of chemotherapy drugs. For now, patients can practice memory-building exercises to counter the effects of this condition. In addition, increasing patient awareness about the condition might be the best way to prevent people from feeling isolated and depressed, and encourage them to seek early treatment.

effects a patient may expect must be weighed against their potential to disrupt his or her life. For example, when professional cyclist Lance Armstrong was diagnosed with testicular cancer in 1996, his chemotherapy regimen was designed with its effect on his career in mind. Ordinarily, early stage testicular cancer can be treated surgically—the diseased testicle is removed. In Armstrong's case, however, the cancer had already spread to his lungs and brain and required chemotherapy. The most important objective, of course, was Armstrong's survival; after that, however, Armstrong wanted to preserve his career. This secondary goal, given the side effects of the drugs he would have to take, was harder to achieve.

Armstrong found medical oncologist Lawrence Einhorn, one of the country's top testicular cancer specialists. Together, they worked carefully to find a treatment that would let Armstrong return to professional cycling. Despite its potential side effects, chemotherapy was preferable to the only other remaining option, radiation therapy. Radiation therapy was avoided because one side effect would have been a slight loss of balance. To the average person, this balance loss hardly would be detectable, but to an athlete like Armstrong, it could mean the end of a career.

The chemotherapy regimen that Einhorn had developed typically involved a combination of several potent drugs. In Armstrong's case, some substitutions had to be made in the normal course of medications to alleviate future side effects. For example, one of the drugs Einhorn usually used, bleomycin, had mild side effects but also lowered the patient's lung capacity—a huge problem for a professional cyclist. The replacement drug, ifosfamide, had no effect on the lungs but had more immediate side effects, such as extreme nausea. Armstrong decided to suffer through a more uncomfortable treatment for the long-term benefit.

Suffering from testicular cancer, Lance Armstrong underwent aggressive chemotherapy. The treatment was a success, and Armstrong is today one of the world's top cyclists.

Despite its drawbacks, chemotherapy was not optional in Armstrong's case. As Einhorn explains, "This disease [testicular cancer] grows so very rapidly that if you fail to kill all the cancer with chemotherapy, it doesn't come back years later, it comes back months later. When a patient is one year cancer-free after chemotherapy, he has a ninety-five percent probability of a cure."[22]

In addition to chemotherapy, Armstrong needed surgery to remove a secondary tumor from his brain. As a result of the surgery and four separate five-day courses of chemotherapy, Armstrong lost fifteen pounds and most of his hair fell out. He suffered through nausea and vomiting that left him feeling weak and listless. In the end, though, Armstrong was still cancer-free in October 1997, one year after his first chemotherapy treatment. Thanks to careful use of chemotherapy, Armstrong did more than survive. He went on to win professional cycling's most prestigious race, the Tour de France, in 1999, 2000, 2001, 2002, and again in 2003.

Fighting Fire with Fire

As Lance Armstrong's story illustrates, it is important that doctors not only fully understand the side effects of particular chemotherapy drugs before administering them to patients but that they keep their patients' other needs in mind as they design a treatment regimen. With hundreds of available drugs, each one slightly different, doctors have wide options when choosing a drug regimen to minimize discomfort in a patient's life. Still, work continues to improve chemotherapy drugs by further reducing unwanted side effects.

Among the most serious side effects researchers have sought to eliminate is the tendency of some drugs to cause the very disease they are meant to cure. Many traditional chemotherapy drugs have the potential to actually cause cancer if administered improperly. These drugs often kill cells by damaging DNA and thereby preventing replication, but their action is by no means restricted to cancer cells. The risk, therefore, is that the DNA of a healthy cell will be damaged and mutate during treatment. Such mutations, in turn, can cause cancer. Since doctors understand these side effects, however, they can often minimize or eliminate them.

Some side effects, such as hair loss, are merely annoying or mildly unpleasant. Others, such as anemia, are often serious and need to be treated with yet more medications. Anemia, in fact, is extremely common: Seven out of ten chemotherapy patients experience this particular symptom. The anemia leads to fatigue that is so extreme that simple things like taking a shower or finishing a meal completely exhaust the patient.

The cause of the fatigue is well understood from a medical standpoint. Since fast-dividing bone marrow cells are often casualties of chemotherapy, fewer and fewer blood cells are produced as chemotherapy continues. Eventually, a patient undergoing chemotherapy is weakened by the loss of these red blood cells, and this exhaustion can interfere with the patient's recovery. According to Gregory Curt, clinical director at the National Cancer Institute and member of the Fatigue Coalition, "The physical, emotional and economic stress of fatigue on cancer patients has a serious impact on their ability to get back to the business of living."[23]

Even though fatigue is frequently a normal part of chemotherapy, studies have shown that only 9 percent of chemotherapy patients suffering from fatigue receive treatment for the condition. The rest of the victims think fatigue is an inevitable and untreatable side effect. "It's like an iceberg sitting there underneath the surface," said Tejpal Grover of the M.D. Anderson Cancer Center in Houston. "It's a lot bigger problem than people seem to appreciate."[24]

For patients with chemotherapy-related anemia, doctors generally prescribe a drug called Procrit, which promotes the development of new red blood cells to replace the ones destroyed by chemotherapy. An

Chemotherapy Drugs and Side Effects

Chemotherapy Drug and *Brand Name(s)*	How Administered	Some Cancer Types Targeted	Some Common Side Effects*
Cisplatin *Platinol®,* *Platinol®-AQ*	IV	Testicular, ovarian, bladder, lung, breast, cervical, stomach, and prostate cancers; Hodgkin's and non-Hodgkin's lymphomas	Nausea and vomiting, kidney problems, low blood counts (increased risk of infection or anemia)
Imatinib mesylate (STI-571) *Gleevec™*	oral/pill	Leukemia, gastrointestinal tumors	Low blood counts (increased risk of infection or anemia), nausea and vomiting, muscle cramps and bone pain, diarrhea, skin rash, fever
Mechlorethamine (nitrogen mustard) *Mustargen®*	IV	Hodgkin's disease and non-Hodgkin's lymphoma; lung and breast cancers	Low blood counts (increased risk of infection or anemia), nausea and vomiting, hair loss, mouth sores, loss of fertility
Methotrexate *Rheumatrex®* *Trexall™*	IV or pill	Breast, head and neck, lung, stomach, and esophagus cancers; leukemia and non-Hodgkin's lymphoma	Low blood counts (increased risk of infection or anemia), mouth sores, nausea and vomiting, poor appetite
Paclitaxel *Taxol®* *Onxal™*	IV	Breast, ovarian, lung, bladder, and prostate cancers; other solid tumor cancers	Hair loss, joint and muscle pain, nausea and vomiting, diarrhea, mouth sores, fever or chills

* side effects experienced by more than 30 percent of patients; most patients do not experience all side effects

Source: www.chemocare.com.

increase in the number of red blood cells gives the patient more strength, which in turn makes the patient more physically able to continue a course of chemotherapy. Procrit, therefore, is often more than just an adjunct to chemotherapy; in severely anemic cancer patients, it is an integral part of the overall drug regimen.

Issues with Immunity

An even greater problem than anemia is impaired immune function, which is also caused by the damage done to bone marrow. The bone marrow, in addition to red blood cells, is responsible for the production of white blood cells. As the number of white blood cells is reduced enormously, a condition known as neutropenia results and the immune system is not as able to protect the body as it used to be. The development of this condition can force doctors to interrupt chemotherapy, which in turn reduces the chances of the patient beating the cancer.

As a result of conditions such as neutropenia, doctors find themselves having to decide how aggressively to fight a cancer. For elderly patients with prostate cancer, for example, a gentler course of chemotherapy is often prescribed, creating an approximately 5 percent chance of neutropenia and the opportunistic infections that go along with it. "On the other end of the extreme," explains Derek Raghavan, chief of medical oncology at the University of Southern California, "patients . . . who have leukemia, or those with aggressive non-Hodgkin's lymphoma or testicular cancer, we push hard with chemotherapy and you might get an infection rate as high as fifty or sixty percent."[25]

The problems posed by neutropenia are illustrated by the case of Chuck Lowe, a sufferer of non-Hodgkin's lymphoma whose chemotherapy brought about a dangerous infection. Said Lowe's son Rob, "While he owes his life to chemotherapy, ten years ago [my father] developed a troubling side effect of the chemo—an infection. It almost devastated him until he got the infection under control."[26]

Desperate Measures

Whatever the side effects of treatment, often cancer sufferers are willing to put up with any amount of discomfort if they will be cured of their disease. When conventional therapies do not work, some patients turn to unconventional and unproven remedies. One such remedy that has become somewhat notorious is known as Hoxley's herbal treatment.

This therapy originated in 1840 as a treatment for a horse with a cancerous sore on its leg. Patients are given a paste of antimony, zinc, bloodroot, arsenic, sulfur, and talc as an external treatment, as well as a liquid cocktail of licorice, red clover, burdock root, *Stillingia* root, barberry, *Cascara*, prickly ash bark, buckthorn bark, and potassium iodide. Additionally, a mixture of procaine hydrochloride, vitamins, liver, and cactus is prescribed for the patient to ingest. Several reports indicate that Hoxley's herbal treatment has no scientific basis for success; furthermore, the ingredients of the remedy are actually thought to cause damage—and sometimes even cause cancer—to healthy tissue upon contact. Nevertheless, this treatment has been used since 1840 and a medical clinic in Tijuana, Mexico, continues to offer the treatment to desperate patients.

When neutropenia compromises the immune system, even something as commonplace as the flu can become life threatening. Cancer patients are already battling one life-threatening disease and are often dealing with complications from chemotherapy and other treatments. The cancer patient's life, then, can become a seemingly endless round of visits to doctors to treat not just the cancer but the myriad infections that can take hold when the immune system is performing at a substandard level.

The customary remedy for chemotherapy-related neutropenia is the administration of compounds known as colony-stimulating drugs. These drugs stimulate the bone marrow into producing more than the normal number of white blood cells. One of the standard colony-stimulating drugs has been filgrastim, which has been marketed under the name Neupogen. In 2002 the FDA approved the use of a second-generation colony-stimulating drug known as pegylated filgrastim, commonly called Neulasta. Neulasta is much more powerful and longer lasting than Neupogen. A single dose of Neulasta has the same overall effect as many injections of Neupogen. According to Gary Lyman of the University of Rochester, "These agents cut the risk of documented infection in half and allow delivery of a full dose of the chemotherapy more often. There is also a fifty percent reduction in the incidence of hospitalization for infection."[27]

A Better Way

In response to the side effects caused by chemotherapy drugs, a whole new field of drug design has been created. These drugs are essentially chemical therapy for chemotherapy. As a result of the development of drugs such as Procrit and Neulasta, chemotherapy has become more effective for cancer patients. With the help of these drugs, patients can receive full courses of treatment.

Treating the side effects of chemotherapy is important, then, not only for the quality of a patient's life but also for his or her survival. If the side effects are unbearable, chemotherapy cannot be administered. In fact, perhaps the strongest driving force behind the development of new chemotherapy drugs is the need for medications that do not cause uncomfortable or potentially lethal side effects. An integral part of this effort is for scientists to gain a clearer understanding of how cancer forms and grows within the body and to pave the way toward developing drugs that target cancer cells more specifically and exclusively.

CHAPTER 5

Genetic Origins, Molecular Cures

Scientists began developing and using chemotherapy drugs to fight cancer in the 1940s, but because the mechanisms by which previously healthy tissue became cancerous were poorly understood, early treatments were relatively nonspecific. Not until the 1970s, in fact, did scientists really begin to understand the true origins of this disease. "Until we knew what was wrong with the cancer cell," says oncologist Bert Vogelstein of Johns Hopkins University, "we couldn't even think about ways of targeting treatment."[28]

Finding the Source

In the 1970s great strides toward understanding cancer on a genetic level were taken, first by Harold Varmus and Mike Bishop in 1970, then by Arnold Levine in 1979. Varmus and Bishop began their research at the University of California at San Francisco with a virus that was known to cause a type of cancer, called a sarcoma, in chickens. Named for the scientist who discovered it, Peyton Rous, the Rous sarcoma virus (RSV) was the first virus with carcinogenic abilities to be identified. However, the way in which RSV caused cancer was unknown. Varmus and Bishop set out to understand this process. They reexamined RSV, this time from a molecular standpoint.

Varmus and Bishop discovered that RSV contained a gene that was almost identical to a normal gene in chickens. The only differences between the viral gene and the normal gene were a few alterations in the genetic sequence. Those few alterations, however, were enough to make the viral gene oncogenic (able to cause cancer). Varmus and Bishop named this gene *src* (for sarcoma). When RSV infected a healthy chicken cell, it turned the cell into a factory that produced viral genes, including the defective form of *src*. The viral *src* is produced in large quantities—much larger than normal chicken *src*. The defective gene interferes with the cell's normal function and makes it divide uncontrollably.

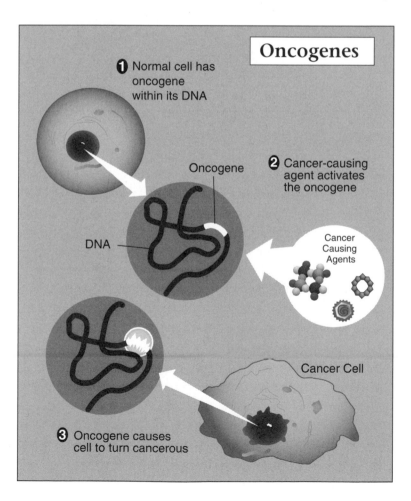

Oncogenes

❶ Normal cell has oncogene within its DNA

Oncogene

❷ Cancer-causing agent activates the oncogene

DNA

Cancer Causing Agents

Cancer Cell

❸ Oncogene causes cell to turn cancerous

The viral *src* gene, which Varmus and Bishop called an oncogene, ultimately causes cancer when produced in large quantities.

The greatest importance of Varmus and Bishop's discovery was the linkage of cancer to mutations in the genetic code. Before their work, it was known that viruses, genes, and chemicals could cause cancer and that chemicals could cause genes to mutate by damaging DNA. By proving the relationship between the normal *src* gene and the mutated, viral *src* gene, Varmus and Bishop had clearly established that mutated genes could cause cells to become cancerous; furthermore, that some viruses, such as RSV, can cause cancer by transmitting mutated genes.

The Other Half of the Problem

Varmus and Bishop's discovery was momentous, but as it turns out, oncogenes are only half the story. Another class of genes, called tumor suppressor genes, also plays an important role in the genetic basis of cancer. When Varmus and Bishop reported their findings, a researcher named Arnold Levine realized that their work did not address aging as another factor in the development of cancer. He wrote:

> There is a thousand-fold increase in the rate or incidence of cancer when comparing a 20-year-old to a 75-year-old. If you smoke, there is a hundred-fold increase. If you have the viruses hepatitis B or hepatitis C, there is an eighty-fold increase. But aging is a thousand-fold increase, so age is clearly one of the four cornerstones for understanding cancer.[29]

Oncogenes, Levine believed, could not explain why aging seemed to play such a role in developing cancer. He believed the solution must lie in another class of genes, different from oncogenes, but a class that still played a role in cancer when mutated.

In 1979 Levine discovered a gene called p53. When the DNA of a cell gets damaged, the p53 gene codes

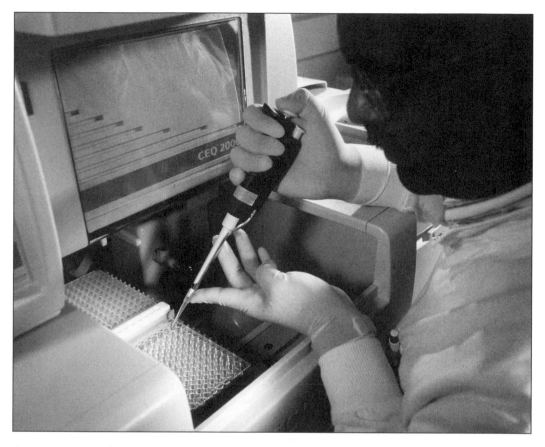

A scientist researches the p53 gene responsible for regulating cellular division and the life span of all cells.

for a protein that prevents damaged DNA from being replicated, and in this way stops unregulated cell division. The gene is also crucial in regulating the life span of a cell, Levine found. Normal cells contain genetically programmed limits on their life spans—in essence, instructions to commit suicide. The proper function of p53 is essential in triggering the cell to respond to signals that tell it to commit suicide.

By 1989, Levine, with the help of another researcher, Bert Vogelstein, had discovered that p53 was a tumor suppressor gene. As Levine described, "Tumor suppressor genes normally prevent cancer and, when mutant, they fail to prevent cancer."[30] When p53 becomes defective, which commonly happens as people age, the cell does not know to stop growing or commit suicide, and cell division becomes virtually uncontrollable. This discovery proved incredibly important to the understanding of cancer; indeed, over time researchers concluded that nearly half of all human cancers involve an error in the p53 protein.

Curtis Harris of the National Cancer Institute has studied how p53 mutates in cancer patients. He has found that mutated p53 genes are involved in various cancers including lung cancer and liver cancer, but that a different defect in p53 is associated with each type of cancer. This suggests that it is not a specific mutation in p53 that causes cancer; rather, any alteration in this protein seems to interfere with its ability to function properly within the machinery of the cell. According to Harris, "If one of [the proteins] develops a kink in its structure, then the machine doesn't fit together as well."[31] This is one of the first steps in the series of events that eventually leads to cancer.

The Cancer Cell Cycle

What the p53 gene does, in essence, is code for the protein that helps control the cell cycle. Early scientists understood the basics of the cell cycle: Cells had to grow, replicate their DNA, then complete division in each round. As people better understood the molecular basis of these cellular events, their knowledge of the cell cycle changed as well. What scientists came to see is that dozens of different genes work to control the cell cycle. It is now known that p53, for example, is a tumor suppressor gene that can stop the cell cycle when it detects DNA damage. On the other hand, the gene that Varmus and Bishop identified, *src*, an oncogene, is involved in countering the action of p53 to allow the erroneous cell division to proceed.

As of 2002, scientists have identified more than one hundred different oncogenes and fifteen different tumor suppressor genes. In the simplest terms, if tumor suppressor genes normally act as brakes, oncogenes act as gas pedals. A mutated tumor suppressor gene is a faulty brake—it cannot stop the cell cycle. A mutated oncogene, on the other hand, is a stuck gas pedal. Defects in either type of gene force the cell cycle to continue even under conditions that normally would halt it. The end result is a cell that cannot and will not stop dividing.

Since cancer is at its heart a genetic problem, understanding the gene or genes that are defective, as well as understanding how the defect forms, is potentially the key to finding a cure. As Columbia University professor and cancer expert I. Bernard Weinstein wrote, "By unraveling the molecular circuitry that maintains the biologic properties of cancer cells, we will be better able to predict selective molecular targets for cancer therapy."[32]

One of the aspects of cancer cells that potentially can be exploited for therapeutic purposes is the fact that they are "addicted to" their genetic anomalies. This is to say that every cancer cell is dependent on the continued expression of the mutated oncogene or tumor suppressor gene. If, for some reason, the mutated gene is no longer expressed, the cancer cell stops dividing and may even commit suicide. Even in advanced forms of cancer, if the expression of the mutated gene is stopped, the patient goes into remission. This realization has led to the development of drugs that target specific genetic anomalies rather than rapidly dividing cells. Better targeting by these designer drugs leads to fewer negative side effects for patients.

One example of such a designer drug is Gleevec, which is used to treat an uncommon cancer, chronic myeloid leukemia (CML), which affects approximately five thousand Americans a year. It causes the bone marrow to produce immature blood cells that are then released into the patient's bloodstream. Eventually, the immature cells crowd out normal white blood cells, red blood cells, and platelets, resulting in anemia, fatigue, and problems with infections and bleeding.

A Rare Leukemia

Compared to the expected 1.3 million new cases of cancer diagnosed in the United States each year, the approximately five thousand cases of CML make it a relatively rare disease. Yet experts consider Gleevec, which is effective against CML and almost nothing else, to be one of the most exciting chemotherapy drugs ever developed.

Like all leukemias, CML affects a patient's bone marrow. Because CML is a blood cancer and therefore does not produce solid tumors, these patients were treated with high doses of traditional chemotherapy, total body irradiation, or bone marrow transplants. Aggressive treatment regimens that involved all of those approaches were the most effective, but even so, fewer than two-thirds of patients survived five years. In many cases of CML, moreover, doctors cannot perform bone marrow transplants because the surgery would be too traumatic for the already infirm patient or because a suitable bone marrow donor could not be found. In these patients, the five-year survival rate drops to less than 50 percent. Before Gleevec, the outlook for CML patients was grim.

The Philadelphia Chromosome

The story of Gleevec began in 1960 in Philadelphia. Two researchers at the University of Pennsylvania, Peter Nowell and David Hungerford, noticed something curious about the chromosomes of CML patients—chromosome 22 was unusually short. Nowell and Hungerford called this shortened chromosome the Philadelphia chromosome.

Scientists already knew that chromosomes sometimes exchange pieces among themselves in a process known as translocation and that this action can lead to defects in a person's genetic code. In the case of the CML patients, 95 percent of the time the disease is linked to an unequal swap of genetic material between chromosomes 9 and 22. At the time, however, Nowell and Hungerford did not know if the exchange was a

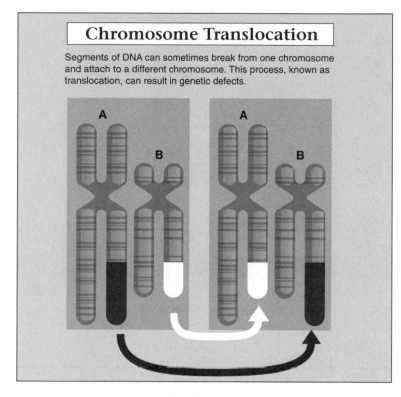

Chromosome Translocation

Segments of DNA can sometimes break from one chromosome and attach to a different chromosome. This process, known as translocation, can result in genetic defects.

cause or an effect of CML. In addition, they did not have the tools to identify which genes were involved in this unequal exchange.

Not until the 1980s did the technology that allows scientists to figure out what genes were swapped in CML patients become available. What researchers found was that the translocation that creates the Philadelphia chromosome also activates the production of a protein involved in helping white blood cells survive. When too much of this protein is produced, potentially life-threatening levels of white blood cells accumulate in the body, causing CML.

Sometimes when a chromosomal translocation takes place, two sequences of DNA that normally code for two different proteins get fused into making one protein. Two researchers at the Massachusetts Institute of Technology, David Baltimore and Owen Witte, found that, in the Philadelphia chromosome, a stretch of DNA that codes for a protein called BCR gets attached to a

A Deadly Combination

At the time that David Baltimore and Owen Witte identified BCR-ABL, they were not planning to cure chronic myeloid leukemia (CML). Witte, a junior researcher in Baltimore's lab at Massachusetts Institute of Technology, was studying a form of leukemia in mice that a virus caused. This virus, the Abelson virus, commandeered the function of a mouse gene called ABL by adding extra genetic material, resulting in the over-stimulation of cell growth.

In 1982 Baltimore and Witte realized that the mice infected with the Abelson virus developed a particular type of leukemia; in fact, they developed CML. Almost immediately, the scientists speculated that the extra genetic material in the Abelson virus, a copy of ABL might correspond to what was happening with the Philadelphia chromosome that was associated with CML in humans.

Baltimore and Witte knew that the normal ABL needed some type of signal to be turned on, whereas the viral version of ABL was constantly active and constantly promoting the production of white blood cells. They looked more closely at the genetic material fused to ABL in the Philadelphia chromosome. They found that that stretch of DNA corresponded to a gene called BCR.

The BCR protein also has a role in communication within the cell, a process called signal transduction. Its biggest job inside of cells is to attach itself to other proteins and act as an *on* switch. The ABL protein is one of the things that BCR activates. When the BCR is fused to ABL, the switch is always on and white blood cells are constantly produced. Active ABL also prevents white blood cells from responding to signals telling them to die when the body detects the excess. If left unchecked, this condition leads to leukemia.

stretch of DNA that codes for a protein called ABL. As a result, a fusion protein called BCR-ABL is produced.

Baltimore and Witte were able to establish that the BCR-ABL fusion protein was responsible for stimulating the constant production of white blood cells and preventing the death of existing white blood cells. In essence, the presence of the fusion protein directly led to the accumulation of white blood cells in CML.

When Baltimore and Witte demonstrated how the Philadelphia chromosome caused CML, it changed the scientific community's understanding of cancer. As Witte explained, "[It] made us realize that cancer did not necessarily result from random chromosome changes and that it could be caused not only by a loss or gain of information, but also by a rearrangement of information."[33]

Stopping the Signal

Baltimore and Witte's work raised the hope that people with the Philadelphia chromosome were not doomed to suffer from CML. The two scientists thought a drug could be designed to target the defective protein and correct the problem the genetic defect caused. They speculated that stopping the hyperactive BCR-ABL protein could stop CML. "I gave a lot of seminars and kept telling people this would be a great target," said Witte.[34] If scientists could make a drug that specifically interfered with the defective protein's signal to manufacture white blood cells (what they called a signal transduction inhibitor) it might be able to stop the progression of CML.

The unusually short chromosome 22 typical of chronic myeloid leukemia patients is clearly visible in this micrograph of a set of chromosomes.

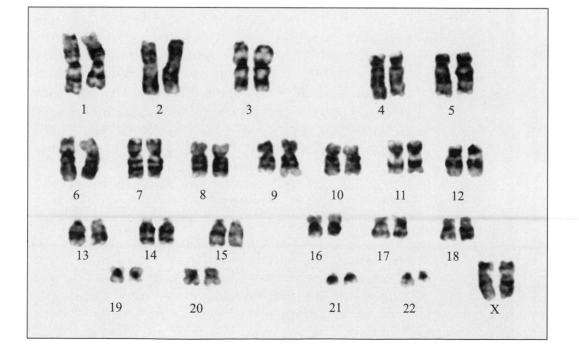

Signal transduction inhibitors, or STIs, are different from traditional chemotherapy drugs in the way they kill cells. Rather than interfering with both normal and cancerous cells' ability to divide, STIs target a specific defect in a specific type of cancer cell—the defects are like bull's-eyes for the STIs to seek out. Normal cells are not killed by STIs because they do not carry the molecular target. In effect, STIs turn a cancer cell into a benign, if not exactly normal, cell.

The Birth of Gleevec

Even as Baltimore and Witte were forming their theory that a signal transduction inhibitor could cure CML, researchers at a company called Novartis Pharmaceuticals were developing and testing hundreds of such substances. Their search, however, was largely for cures for other cancers. They felt that CML was too rare a disease to warrant much attention, and therefore they pursued molecules that are defective in more common cancers.

Brian J. Druker of the Oregon Health Sciences University in Portland was one of the scientists who supplied potential drugs to Novartis. When he heard of Baltimore's and Witte's work, he became interested in an inhibitor the scientists working for Novartis had generated, STI571. This inhibitor, Druker knew, was not potent against the general targets Novartis was interested in, but it was able to specifically stop production of the protein that Baltimore and Witte had shown was responsible for CML.

Druker immediately began work to prove that STI571, or Gleevec, could act on cancer cells while leaving other cells alone. He first tested the drug on animals, then used it on blood samples from CML patients. Clinical trials began in 1998, and almost all of the patients who took Gleevec—fifty-one out of fifty-three—went into total remission with very few side effects. In half those patients, the presence of cancerous cells was nearly undetectable after treatment.

New and Powerful STIs

Gleevec's success against chronic myeloid leukemia and gastrointestinal stromal tumors led researchers to develop other signal transduction inhibitors. One such drug, SU101, seems promising against other cancers. SU101 blocks the signaling of a protein called the platelet-derived growth factor receptor. This protein is thought to be defective in various types of cancer, including that of the brain, prostate, and ovaries.

In early clinical trials, SU101 was able to shrink brain tumors and prolong life in terminally ill patients by three to four months. For some patients cancer has been stabilized for up to two years. Researchers are especially hopeful for SU101 because the drug is able to penetrate the blood-brain barrier (which stands in the way of many traditional chemotherapy drugs) and the side effects are fairly mild.

It was soon discovered that Gleevec was also effective against another disease, an equally rare stomach malignancy called gastrointestinal stromal tumors (GIST). Through subsequent rounds of clinical trials, Gleevec proved so effective that it sailed through the Food and Drug Administration's approval process in a matter of months—faster than any other cancer drug in history. As the FDA's acting commissioner, Bernard A. Schwetz explains, "Although the long term benefits of the drug are not yet known, early studies have shown that Gleevec will offer a significant improvement for many patients."[35]

An Incomplete Cure

"We are gaining more and more control over the cancer problem each year, and [the development of Gleevec] is a particularly graphic demonstration of it," said Baltimore in 2001. "For a drug that has such a dramatic effect on cancer to have such little effect on the whole normal body is miraculous."[36] Indeed, the effects of Gleevec treatments were dramatic. For example, a GIST victim named Trudy Webb was on her deathbed before she started taking Gleevec. A ten-pound tumor in her chest was putting so much pressure on her lungs that even breathing was difficult. She became part of a Gleevec clinical trial as a last resort, and within a week, her tumor began to melt away.

Yet as dramatic as the results could be, Gleevec soon showed weaknesses. The most significant problem was that, sometimes, patients with CML who initially responded well to Gleevec suffered relapses. These relapses, researchers found, were due to cancer cells that had mutated to the point that the protein that signaled white blood cell production was no longer recognizable to the drug. The very strength of Gleevec—that it worked on specific molecular targets and left similar molecules alone—meant that a subtle shift in the structure of a cancer cell's proteins would render the drug useless. The drug might have few or no side effects, but it might also stop working in patients that it had previously cured.

Still, because scientists understood how Gleevec worked and why it stopped working in certain patients, the drug continued to be useful. As Richard Van Etten of the Center for Blood Research explained:

> We've gone from finding STI-571, to using it in patients, to seeing the resistance, to understanding the responsible mutations—all within about three years. . . . There is good news and bad news here. . . . The bad news is that developing resistance to Gleevec in advanced CML is a common problem and that mutations in BCR-ABL may be the major cause. The good news is that BCR-ABL is still a valid target for therapy in resistant patients, and understanding these mutations will be essential in designing approaches to overcome resistance or avoid it altogether.[37]

Although the Gleevec story did not end with a sure-fire cure for a type of cancer, it was still an important milestone in the history, and the future, of chemotherapy. Gleevec was one of the first examples of the kind of anticancer drug that scientists have been dreaming about for decades: effective, specific, deadly, and target-specific. Using the Gleevec model, researchers continue to develop drugs for other cancers.

CHAPTER 6

An Alternative Approach

For the most part, chemotherapy has always aimed to kill diseased cells. From traditional chemical poisons to more recent molecular-level treatments, the cancer cell itself had always been the target. In the 1960s, however, some scientists decided to take a revolutionary approach to chemotherapy. They no longer limited chemotherapy to agents that could act specifically against the cancer cell. Instead, they believed that any tactic that could keep cancer from killing its victim should be explored as thoroughly as methods that directly targeted tumors. The result of this new way of thinking was the development of a new class of drugs. These drugs, called angiogenesis inhibitors, attacked and killed normal cells to starve out cancerous ones.

The Problem with Blood

As with other advances in chemotherapy, the development of angiogenesis inhibitors was the outgrowth of work initially unrelated to cancer research. In 1961 the navy began using nuclear-powered aircraft carriers, fully self-sufficient and able to stay at sea for months at a time. There was only one problem: The ship's blood supply could be stored only for three weeks. Realizing that the vessels would be useless as long-term floating military bases without a long-lasting blood supply, the navy asked a young doctor named Judah Folkman to figure out a better way to store blood for extended periods of time.

Folkman found a way to dry out the blood for storage, then reconstitute it with saline solution when it was needed. To test whether this process actually resulted in usable blood, Folkman set up a crude circulatory system connected to a rabbit thyroid. If the reconstituted blood was as good as regular blood, the thyroid tissue would stay alive—and sure enough, it did.

Just to be thorough, Folkman decided to test whether the reconstituted blood also could be used to support new tissue growth. Remembering that cancer cells are among the fastest growing types of cells, he injected them into the thyroid to see if they would grow when supplied with the experimental blood. Tumors sprang up all over the thyroid, suggesting the blood was functional. Then, unexpectedly, the tumors stopped growing.

"We thought maybe [the cancer cells] died," explained Folkman. "And so, to see if they died, we . . . took them out of the thyroid gland and put them back into . . . mice."[38] The cancer cells came back to life inside the lab mice and were able to cause tumors to appear and to grow.

Folkman concluded that both the reconstituted blood and the cancer cells were normal. Therefore, there must have been something about

Judah Folkman's discovery that tumors cannot grow without a blood supply led to the creation of drugs that inhibit the growth of new blood cells.

the artificial setup that prevented the cancer cells from growing in the thyroid. Folkman then recognized the crucial difference between the tumors in the mice and the tumors on the thyroid gland. He explained: "In the mouse we found many, many blood vessels had come into the tumor, and in the thyroid gland there seemed to be no vessels growing into the tumor."[39] Based on this information, Folkman formed a theory that said that tumors could not grow without a blood supply, and that angiogenesis, the process by which new blood vessels grow, is the key to tumor expansion.

Angiogenesis is a normal part of the healing process, when blood vessels are required to grow into newly forming tissue. The blood vessels bring nutrients without which the tissue could not continue to develop. In cancer, excessive angiogenesis occurs to feed tumors, allowing them to grow rapidly. In addition, all the blood vessels running through the tumor make it easier for the cancer to metastasize—cancer cells can dislodge from the original tumor, escape into circulation and take root in other parts of the body.

Folkman theorized that by stopping the development of new blood vessels, tumor growth could also be stopped. Essentially, he suggested starving out cancer tumors. Folkman was virtually alone in his newfound interest. While everyone else in the field of cancer research was looking inside the cancer cell to solve the mystery of the disease, Folkman was the only one looking at the blood vessels that gave cancer life.

Many scientists thought Folkman's ideas were ridiculous, commenting that they saw no blood vessels in the tumors they studied. Folkman replied based on his experience as a surgeon. He explains, "I had seen and handled cancers and they were hot and red and bloody. . . . I knew [my critics] were looking at tumors that had been taken out [of the body]. All the blood was drained. They were specimens."[40]

Promoting Starvation

It took years of research before Folkman convinced his scientific colleagues that angiogenesis occurred in tumors and that the process was important in tumor growth. It took years more to isolate the biochemical components that were responsible for a tumor's ability to promote blood vessel formation. As soon as that was done, however, the investigation shifted from looking for factors that help angiogenesis to those that can inhibit angiogenesis.

Folkman and his colleague Michael O'Reilly began the search for angiogenesis inhibitors inside the human body.

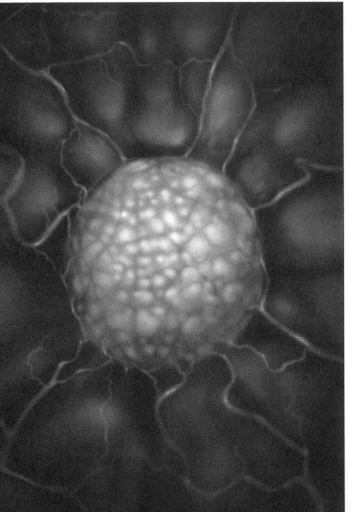

Blood vessels nourish a tumor. Blood vessels not only promote tumor growth, but they also serve as conduits for the tumor to spread to other parts of the body.

As they searched, Folkman and O'Reilly made the minimization of side effects part of their goal. Overall, there is less of a concern about general toxicity with angiogenesis inhibitors, as they prevent growth of blood vessels rather than killing or preventing the division of cells, but the possible involvement of the immune system must be considered. Angiogenesis inhibitors differ from other chemotherapy drugs in that they are often proteins rather than chemicals. When new proteins are introduced into the body, there is a possibility that the immune system will label them as invaders. An immune response follows, disabling the protein and preventing any therapeutic effects. For this reason, researchers hoped to find an inhibitor that was normally used by the

An Old Hobby

Judah Folkman's interest in the relationship between blood and healthy tissue started at a tender age. In high school, he designed an experiment for the school science fair in which he answered the question of how long a rat's heart could be kept alive artificially with cow's blood. In the basement of his home, he and a friend attached an electric motor and a bicycle pump to tubes running into the rat's heart. Using his sister's toy oven as an incubator, Folkman kept the blood and some saline solution at normal body temperature.

The experiment worked—Folkman was able to keep the heart alive for days. He stayed up all night and even cut classes to look after his research project. In the end, that effort won Folkman recognition: The Ohio Academy of Sciences awarded him and his friend a prize in the annual competition.

body, since such a substance would be less likely to generate an immune response. As Noël Bouk, professor of microbiology at Northwestern University Medical School, explains, "You are not going to have antibodies or unusual reactions against them."[41]

Folkman and O'Reilly named the first drug they found Angiostatin: *angio* for blood vessels, *statin* for stop. Angiostatin was actually a small part of a larger protein that is usually made by tumors. This seeming paradox, that tumors—which require excessive angiogenesis to survive—would also produce angiogenesis inhibitors, is explained by the fact that one way a fast-growing tumor makes sure it gets all the nutrients it needs from the bloodstream is by preventing angiogenesis in other parts of the body. Even other, smaller tumors, are suppressed by these substances.

With the understanding of a tumor's ability to produce its own angiogenesis inhibitors, O'Reilly began the process of isolating Angiostatin. He turned to an unusual source—the urine of cancer-ridden mice. When the body makes too much of anything, the excess usually ends up in the urine. O'Reilly gathered laboratory mice with large primary tumors and began collecting their urine, in the hope that he could isolate

Michael O'Reilly (pictured) worked closely with Judah Folkman to create a drug to inhibit angiogenesis, the process by which new blood cells are formed.

some substance from the urine that had anti-angiogenic properties. For two years, O'Reilly amassed gallons of mouse urine, then purified it drop by drop. At the end, he was left with Angiostatin.

Once they knew what to look for, Folkman and O'Reilly were able to find Angiostatin in human blood as well. Using human blood that had been discarded by the Red Cross because it was no longer viable, they began the arduous process of extracting the human form of the protein to use in laboratory tests on lab mice.

In mice with lung cancer, Angiostatin showed remarkable effects. One hundred percent of the mice treated with Angiostatin were cancer-free after fifteen days. As expected, all of the untreated mice still had extensive lung cancer and were dead in the same amount of time. A year later, Folkman and O'Reilly discovered a second angiogenesis inhibitor (another substance that the human body normally produces) that they called Endostatin.

Both Angiostatin and Endostatin worked just as Folkman had envisioned; they had absolutely no effect on cancer cells directly. Instead, they slowed or stopped new blood vessel formation in and around tumors. Armed with the initial results from animal experiments, researchers began human clinical trials with angiogenesis inhibitors.

Management by Containment

One of the first candidates in an angiogenesis inhibitor clinical trial was Duane Gay, who had extensive cancer in his lungs as well as a large tumor in his liver. Gay had gone through several rounds of surgery and months of traditional chemotherapy, but his cancer had continued to grow. After the first six months of the Endostatin trial, many of Gay's tumors shrunk in size. Those that did not shrink also did not get any bigger, which was a real improvement over what traditional chemotherapy had accomplished. The cancer was not gone, but it was not growing either. By preventing further blood vessel formation, Endostatin effectively stabilized Gay's cancer. Furthermore, since the vessels supplying blood to an untreated patient's tumor are constantly dying off and being replaced by new ones, treatment with Endostatin meant that over time the tumor's blood supply diminished, and the tumor itself would shrink.

For Gay and patients like him, a stable disease is a victory because it means the cancer is not doing any additional damage. As one of the members of Folkman's original team, Don Ingber, explains,

> [Endostatin] offers an opportunity to manage cancer rather than cure cancer, and I think that's the future. It's one that is going to be more like tuberculosis was years ago. It wasn't a complete, immediate cure, but it was managed, and progressively over time became really something that's a smaller part of our fears in life.[42]

The patients taking Endostatin had a better chance of survival even though they technically still had cancer.

A New Use for Thalidomide

Angiostatin and Endostatin were successful angiogenesis inhibitors and proved the value of Folkman's approach. Despite their effectiveness, however, scientists continued to search for other angiogenesis inhibitors that were more effective or that worked on different types of tumors. Just as with other classes of chemotherapy drugs, researchers believed a larger arsenal would be more effective in fighting an array of cancers.

While O'Reilly was working on Angiostatin and Endostatin, other members of Folkman's team concentrated on other areas of angiogenesis research. For example, when Robert D'Amato began working for Folkman, instead of searching for new compounds, he focused on re-evaluating existing drugs that could potentially inhibit angiogenesis. D'Amato speculated that a drug intended for some other disease with the side effect of blocking blood vessel growth might already exist.

One of the drugs D'Amato looked at was Thalidomide, which already had an infamous history. Originally, Thalidomide was found to be effective at combating nausea and was prescribed often in the early 1960s for pregnant women to treat morning sickness. Unfortunately, Thalidomide quickly proved disastrous, since it caused severe birth defects, including incompletely formed or missing limbs, in otherwise normal fetuses. Thousands of babies were born missing arms, legs, or both before use of the drug was discontinued completely.

The attribute in Thalidomide that caused such deformities was its suppression of angiogenesis. D'Amato demonstrated that one form of Thalidomide could inhibit angiogenesis in animal tumors. Since the drug already existed, clinical trials in human cancer patients began immediately. The first patient had multiple myeloma (a common cancer of the bone marrow) and was treated with Thalidomide in 1997. Eighty-three more cancer sufferers for whom standard chemotherapy had failed quickly followed. The researchers conducting the trial defined a response as no progression of the disease or fewer diseased cells in the blood. Overall, the response rate was 32 percent, an impressive response rate for this type of cancer.

Impressive Advantages

As scientists anticipated, angiogenesis inhibitors like Endostatin, which are based on naturally occurring molecules, have many advantages. One strong advantage is the absence of side effects. From an evolutionary standpoint, Endostatin has been around for 600 million years. Something that the human body has kept around for that long is not likely to be toxic in the doses necessary to see effects on tumors. Even patients who

Thalidomide's Miracles

Tim Dawson was one of the first recipients of thalidomide therapy in 1997. Dawson had multiple myeloma, a disease with only two known treatments: traditional chemotherapy and bone marrow transplant. He had tried them both, and both had failed.

Before his doctor, Bart Barlogie, suggested it, Dawson had never heard of Thalidomide. As Dawson explains in a Public Broadcasting Service documentary titled "Cancer Warrior," "I didn't realize it was the drug that caused all the problems, all the birth defects. And I couldn't figure out how that was going to work." Still, he started on the highest dose of the drug—sixteen capsules every day.

Within four weeks, Dawson was feeling much better, and his doctors noticed he looked better as well. His blood work started to come back normal. Barlogie declared that Dawson was in remission.

Dawson still takes Thalidomide and has been in remission for more than a year. His side effects are minimal: He tires easily and feels some numbness and tingling in his fingers and toes. Overall, though, he is happy with the results, as he says, "I can still do things that are normal, and probably without Thalidomide I couldn't do that. I don't know where I'd be if I didn't have it."

have been taking Endostatin for more than eight months do not experience any side effects, whereas patients taking traditional chemotherapy drugs often experience negative side effects right away.

A second powerful advantage of angiogenesis inhibitors in general is that cancers do not seem to build up drug resistance as they do with many other chemotherapy drugs. This is because these drugs target normal endothelial cells, which line the inside of blood vessels. Endothelial cells typically do not mutate, so it is unlikely that drugs will become ineffective due to genetic changes in the target cells. This means patients can take the drugs over long periods of time, and even when a cancer endures the tumor does not grow to the point that it interferes with vital functions.

Another advantage of angiogenesis inhibitors is that they are highly specific to certain types of blood vessels. Researchers have been able to select those compounds that inhibit angiogenesis in tumors without interfering with normal angiogenesis. According to Folkman, "It has always been assumed that wound angiogenesis, tumor angiogenesis, eye angiogenesis were the same—that new vessels were new vessels; there was no difference."[43] From new work in Folkman's lab, it is now well understood that different molecules play roles in blood vessel growth in different parts of the body. Endostatin, for example, mainly turns off angiogenesis in tumors; it has no effect whatsoever on wound healing.

An Expensive Proposition

Despite their proven effectiveness, few anti-angiogenesis drugs are actually available to patients. Part of the problem is cost. The inhibitors are proteins, and pharmaceutical companies do not have a lot of experience producing large quantities of proteins so drug production is expensive and slow. Many pharmaceutical companies prefer to avoid committing billions of dol-

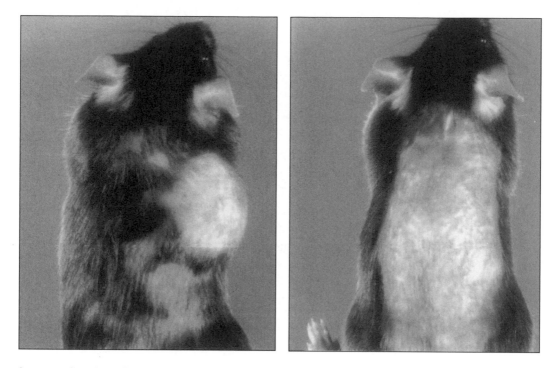

lars to the development of anti-angiogenesis drugs that might not prove successful or profitable.

Another hurdle for anti-angiogenesis research has to do with the model that the medical establishment uses to evaluate anticancer drugs. In order for the FDA and physicians to consider a chemotherapy drug effective, tumors have to shrink or disappear within a few days or weeks. Merely stopping the growth of a tumor, as angiogenesis inhibitors are most likely to do, does not meet the criteria to be considered successful in a clinical trial. Additionally, since angiogenesis inhibitors do not work directly on the tumors themselves, it often takes as long as a few months to see effects. "Chemotherapy guidelines which have been used for the past fifty years are not as useful in anti-angiogenic therapy," said Folkman.[44] The president of a pharmaceutical company that is involved in developing angiogenesis inhibitors adds that the way the FDA tests drugs works against angiogenesis inhibitors:

This mouse's tumor (left) is considerably smaller after being treated with Endostatin (right), an angiogenesis inhibitor.

Preclinically, we see that angiogenesis inhibitors are most effective in early disease and minimal residual disease, but . . . the Food and Drug Administration requires that early testing is done in late-stage disease. If you want to test in early-stage disease, you have to add your drug [into a] standard of care, and then that is another level of difficulty because much of the standard of care is chemotherapy that brings toxicity.[45]

Patients of anti-angiogenesis treatments, however, are being helped. Folkman related one case study of a patient who was living a normal life even though there were still relatively large tumors inside her body: "She had been told she was terminally ill, and her heart had begun to fail. . . . After two months on [Endostatin] she starts to feel better. She develops a tremendous appetite, and goes eight months with [a] stable disease. . . . At 1.5 years, she's at 46 percent regression."[46] This patient's tumors were shrinking, but very slowly, and she was living a relatively normal life. Nonetheless, even a 46 percent tumor regression would not be considered a partial response in a standard cancer trial.

In 2001 the American Society of Clinical Ontology decided that the requirements for success in chemotherapy trials had to be changed. The time frame for observing effects would have to be extended, and the requirement for tumor reduction would be eliminated. Rather, success would be measured by the rate at which tumors are confined and by how long patients can avoid traditional chemotherapy. As anti-angiogenesis trials are standardized and researchers can compare results to real world benefits for cancer patients, experts believe it is likely that angiogenesis inhibitors will emerge as a powerful weapon in the fight against cancer.

CHAPTER 7

Smart Bombs

Once the genetic origins of cancer were firmly established, researchers began working to identify the genetic anomalies that corresponded to the different forms of the disease. If a gene was connected to a certain type of cancer, the hope was to find a drug to target that gene. Said Memorial Sloan-Kettering Cancer Center oncologist Alan Houghton, "The life and death of cells is being worked out, and the dozens and dozens of molecules in the body that participate in those pathways are now becoming targets for therapy."[47]

A variety of approaches were explored to combat cancer with molecular-level chemotherapy. Researchers aimed to create safer, smarter, better drugs, and work proceeded on multiple fronts. By the 1990s, the era of molecular smart bombs had begun.

The Antibody Philosophy

In 1986 two men who were waiting in an airport struck up a conversation. It turned out that they shared similar interests about cancer. Their names were Axel Ullrich, who worked at a pharmaceutical company called Genentech, and Dennis Slamon, an oncologist at the University of California at Los Angeles. As a result of their chance encounter, Ullrich and Slamon began a collaboration that resulted in a major breakthrough in breast cancer research.

Ullrich was primarily interested in oncogenes and their roles in different cancers; Slamon, on the other hand, was a breast cancer researcher who had access to a large number of specimens. Together, they screened Ullrich's oncogenes against Slamon's specimens and discovered that a gene called HER-2/neu was critical in the growth of certain breast cancers.

Patients whose breast cancer is characterized by too many copies of the HER-2/neu gene are referred to as HER-2 positive. When too much of this gene resides or collects inside a cell—in the case of breast cancer patients, between 1 and 2 million copies of HER-2/neu instead of the normal amount of twenty thousand to one hundred thousand—the cell begins dividing uncontrollably, a typical characteristic of cancer. About 30 percent of breast cancers have this particular genetic anomaly, and the resultant cancer is especially hard to treat. Once this type of cancer spreads, patients usually have less than a year to live.

Scientists at Genentech, in collaboration with Slamon, soon developed a drug to target HER-2 positive breast cancers. They used the overexpression of the HER-2/neu gene as a target and developed an antibody against it. They called this antibody drug Herceptin.

Herceptin is a monoclonal antibody, a type of protein the immune system uses to identify, target, and destroy invading organisms and diseased cells. As part of the body's immune response, monoclonal antibodies are generated to target specific infections. By restricting the monoclonal antibodies to recognize only one protein, the body makes sure normal cells are not affected. By design, the immune response fights disease without side effects. Herceptin was not an antibody the body normally made, but its biochemical properties are the same as other monoclonal antibodies—it only recognizes HER-2/neu proteins.

Herceptin attacks cancer cells on many levels. It directly targets the HER-2/neu proteins on a cancer cell and prevents it from dividing. In this way, when a tumor is treated with Herceptin, it cannot continue to grow.

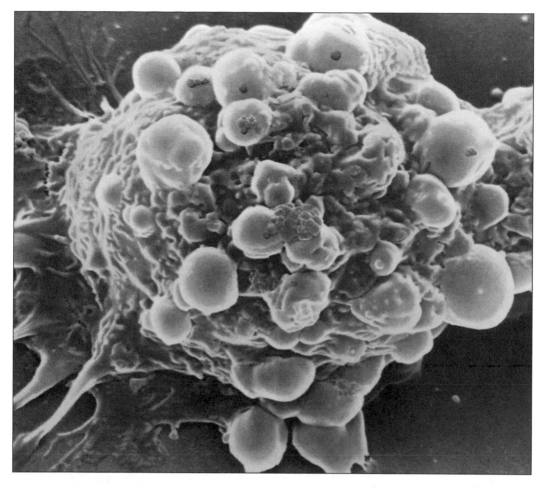

In addition to blocking growth, Herceptin is able to alert the body's immune system to the presence of a cancer cell. When the drug binds to the HER-2/neu receptor, it acts like a red flag waving on the surface of a cancer cell. Certain immune system cells called natural killer cells can detect this red flag. As a result, the cancer cell is no longer invisible to the immune system. The body recognizes it as a disease-causing cell that should be eliminated.

A breast cancer cell containing too many copies of the HER-2/neu gene divides uncontrollably.

Guided Missiles

After Herceptin was developed, Slamon began clinical trials using the drug. The participants in the trial were invariably very sick women. One of the first patients was Barbara Bradfield, who had already undergone surgery, radiation, and chemotherapy— all to no avail. The prospect of more chemotherapy scared Bradfield. "I thought I was probably going to die," she explains, "and I didn't want to die bald and throwing up."[48]

Slamon used Herceptin in combination with traditional chemotherapy on Bradfield's cancer. The results were dramatic. Sixteen tumors on her lungs disappeared, and eight years later, she was still in remission.

Herceptin is not a universal miracle cure, even for patients with Bradfield's type of breast cancer. Overall, however, Herceptin slows the progression of metastatic breast cancer, and when it is combined with Taxol,

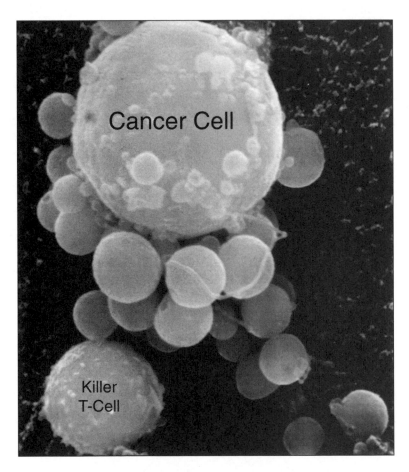

A natural killer cell, or T-cell, attacks a cancer cell treated with the antibody drug, Herceptin. The drug helps the immune system target cancer cells for elimination.

a traditional chemotherapy drug, a study showed that 42 percent of women with metastatic breast cancer saw their tumors shrink by 50 percent or more. With Taxol alone, only 16 percent of patients saw improvements in their cancer. Clearly, Herceptin has real value to cancer patients.

Using the same principles, other monoclonal antibodies have been developed to treat other cancers. For example, the drug Rituxan is targeted to a protein found on B-cell lymphomas, and it is successful in shrinking tumors in 50 percent of patients. Just as Herceptin targets breast cancer cells, Rituxan is expected to have little or no effect on any type of cell other than lymphoma cancer cells.

The Best of Both Worlds

As Bradfield's case illustrates, antibody-based chemotherapy offers a unique and powerful way to target and kill cancer cells. Something as small as a single defective protein is transformed into a detectable target when the antibody system works properly. The body's immune system is alerted to the presence of cancer cells; alternatively, the antibodies are linked to substances toxic to the diseased cells. These substances can be actual chemotherapy drugs attached to an antibody, which can then be delivered specifically to cancer cells to eradicate them. For example, the FDA approved a drug called Mylotarg in 2000 to treat patients with acute myeloid leukemia (AML). Mylotarg contains a highly specific antibody that recognizes special AML cell proteins linked to a potent chemotherapy agent known as calicheamicin. Mylotarg has proven very effective in clinical trials with minimal side effects.

The drawback, however, is that some cancers do not respond as well to chemotherapy, regardless of how directly the drug is administered, as they do to other forms of treatment such as radiation therapy. In light of this fact, a new type of drug called radioimmunotherapy has been designed. Instead of linking the antibody

Success with Bexxar

When Patricia Haut was forty-four years old, she discovered she had a form of B-cell lymphoma. The disease progresses slowly, but in most patients it eventually proves fatal. Haut initially responded to traditional chemotherapy, but the remissions were short-lived. In fact, after each course of chemotherapy, it seemed that Haut's remissions grew shorter and shorter.

In 1993 Haut enrolled in a clinical trial at the University of Michigan. There, Dr. Mark Kaminski was testing a drug called Bexxar, a monoclonal antibody loaded with radioactive iodine. Haut thought Bexxar might be the best weapon against her cancer. She received four infusions of Bexxar over five weeks. In the end, the tumors in her abdomen, chest, and groin disappeared. Ten years later, she remains cancer-free.

to a chemotherapy drug, it is linked to a radioactive substance. In the words of Leo Gordon, professor of hematology and oncology at Northwestern University in Chicago, these new drugs combine "the targeting of a monoclonal antibody with the cancer-killing ability of radiation."[49]

At least two radioimmunotherapy drugs, Zevalin and Bexxar, are currently available for non-Hodgkin's lymphoma patients. Both drugs have proven extremely effective in clinical trials. In 75 percent of patients treated with Zevalin, tumors shrank significantly; in fact, tumors seem to have disappeared in between 15 and 30 percent of the patients. In the case of Bexxar, all patients in the initial study saw their tumors shrink by at least 50 percent; in nearly half of those patients, there were no detectable cancer cells after treatment.

Among the advantages of radioimmunotherapy is the shorter course of treatment. While chemotherapy often is administered over weeks or months, Zevalin and Bexxar are given in only two shots: A test shot to make sure the cancer will respond is followed by a therapeutic dose a week later.

Since these drugs are relatively new to the market, it is not yet known what kind of long-term benefits or disadvantages will result from their use. Scientists are hopeful that this form of therapy will live up to its initial expectations and offer cures for those patients for whom other treatments have failed.

An Infectious Approach

The common lesson drugs like Herceptin, Mylotarg, and Zevalin taught was that attributes of the immune system could be efficiently exploited to treat cancer. Once scientists realized this, everything from viruses to vaccines became potential chemotherapy vehicles. Just as signal transduction inhibitors and anti-angiogenesis agents represented new frontiers in chemotherapy, immunotherapy was recognized as yet another unexplored but potentially valuable area of research.

Laboratory-synthesized antibodies were only one part of immunotherapy for cancer. Some scientists have attempted to use viruses to target cancer cells, using the viruses' own biology to effect the cure. Like other approaches to chemotherapy, this one relies on work that was done years earlier and which then languished. In 1968 a researcher named Laszlo Csatary used a weakened strain of Newcastle disease virus to treat a case of metastatic stomach cancer. The cancer was cured, and Csatary continued researching the use of viruses against cancer for the rest of his career. Yet even though Csatary published his results in respected medical journals, for the most part, the research was ignored for many years.

Decades later, Frank McCormick was one of the first people to rediscover the value of viruses in cancer therapy. Csatary had not used genetically engineered viruses to treat cancer, but he had established the value of viral infections in the treatment of the disease. Still, when McCormick told people about his idea of using a genetically engineered virus to infect and kill cancer cells, most of them dismissed it.

Using solid (if somewhat forgotten) science as a basis, McCormick chose to alter a specific type of virus—an adenovirus—for his cancer treatment. Naturally occurring adenoviruses cause a number of human diseases, including the common cold. Using genetic engineering, McCormick and his team designed an adenovirus to target cells with defects in the p53 tumor suppressor gene. The p53 gene was a natural target because it is involved in so many different types of cancer. Rather than taking a gene therapy approach, McCormick's plan was to exploit the p53 deficiency. "We're not delivering a gene," McCormick explains. "We're actually using the lack of p53 to allow a virus to grow and kill cells."[50]

In 2001, McCormick's company, Onyx Pharmaceuticals, unveiled ONYX-015, a genetically engineered virus that does exactly what McCormick envisioned. The anticancer

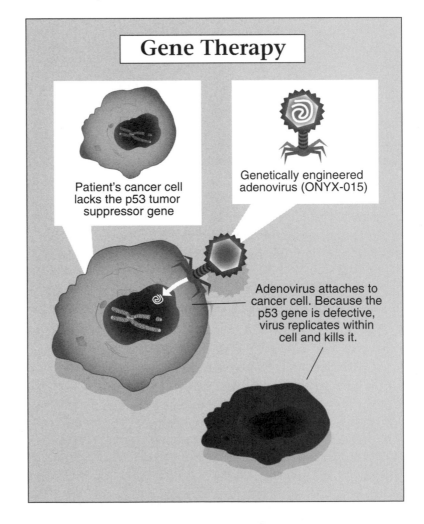

Gene Therapy

Patient's cancer cell lacks the p53 tumor suppressor gene

Genetically engineered adenovirus (ONYX-015)

Adenovirus attaches to cancer cell. Because the p53 gene is defective, virus replicates within cell and kills it.

virus that McCormick created relies on a bit of trickery to do its job. If ONYX-015 infects a normal cell with normal p53, that normal gene blocks the virus from replicating. This essentially renders the virus ineffective in normal cells, and prevents the virus from killing healthy cells. On the other hand, when ONYX-015 infects a cancerous cell in which p53 is defective, there is nothing to impede the virus from replicating within the cancer cell and eventually killing it.

In preliminary clinical trials, ONYX-015 has been used to treat more than three hundred patients and has proven fairly effective against certain types of cancer. Tumors were directly injected with ONYX-015, and researchers reported numerous patients with significant reductions in tumor size and a fair number with undetectable numbers of cancer cells following treatment. The side effects that were reported were minor, including flu-like symptoms, fever, and slight pain at the site of injection. Based on the initial success of ONYX-015, additional therapeutic viruses are being developed to target other gene defects. "There's a whole range of different approaches being used using different agents, different virus vectors and different kinds of indications," says McCormick. "Over the next few years we'll see exactly how safe and efficacious these kinds of treatments are."[51]

Preventive

No matter how sophisticated the approach, chemotherapy is primarily aimed at curing cancer once a person has developed the disease. To a greater or lesser extent, drugs such as ONYX-015 achieve this goal. Still, a person whose cancer is in remission always runs the risk of the cancer reappearing and gaining a new foothold that might be more troublesome than the original disease. For this reason, chemotherapy drugs are sometimes administered for a period of time after a patient appears to be cancer-free. This way, single diseased cells that survive the initial treatment are killed before they can cause a new tumor to develop. The best solution, however, would be to stop a cancer before it ever takes hold. In other words, scientists hope that they might someday develop a cancer vaccine.

For the time being, the focus of cancer vaccine research is on developing therapeutic vaccines. These vaccines, in other words, are not yet used to prevent cancer; rather, they treat the disease in patients for whom other therapies have failed to work. It is a common misconception that vaccines only act to prevent disease—from a strict scientific standpoint, a vaccine is an agent that produces an immune response, irrespective of its timing in relation to the onset of the disease.

One example of a therapeutic vaccine is CanVaxin, which is aimed at the form of skin cancer known as melanoma. CanVaxin was made from cancer cells from three different patients in an effort to represent a variety of tumors. When CanVaxin is administered after surgical removal of tumors, patients have a better chance of survival because the vaccine is able to prompt the body to produce an immune response that kills the remaining cancer cells. According to Guy Gammon, a

Targeted but Not Miraculous

The trend in chemotherapy research is toward finding ever more precisely targeted therapies. The problem with such precision targeting, however, is that a large number of such drugs fail in late-stage clinical trials. Often these failures do not surprise experts. The problem lies in the definition of the word *target*. Drug companies refer to the target as a molecule associated with cancer that can be recognized by a drug in a laboratory setting, but they often ignore the fact that molecules change inside living cells. It is possible that a drug targets the wrong form of a molecule and is ineffective against cancer.

In the Mignon Fogarty article titled "The Reality of Targeted Therapies," which appeared in a 2002 issue of *Scientist*, Brian J. Druker is quoted saying, "I'm very careful with the use of the term 'molecularly targeted.' Every single chemotherapy agent we have is molecularly targeted. Just because you know the target, doesn't make something a good drug."

vice president at CancerVax, the biotech company that makes CanVaxin, "What we've been able to show is that not only do a majority of patients make an immune response, but that those making a strong response survive longer."[52]

Scientists at Stanford University have also reported success using other therapeutic cancer vaccines against colon and lung cancer. In 2001 vaccines tailor-made for each patient using their own cells combined with proteins found on colon and lung tumors were able to shrink the tumors even in advanced cases. According to lead researcher Lawrence Fong, "Our hope is to make these vaccines more potent and to try them in earlier-stage disease, possibly even using them to prevent disease."[53]

Drawbacks and Deficiencies

Despite the benefits of these immunotherapy cancer drugs, they are not panaceas. A number of factors can impair the ability of these drugs to treat cancer. For example, just as cancer's tendency to mutate can render other highly targeted drugs ineffective, the high specificity of antibodies becomes a disadvantage if the target on the cancer cell mutates even slightly. Unfortunately for cancer patients, there is a high probability of such mutations. According to Frank Rauscher III of the Wistar Cancer Center in Philadelphia, "Once you have diagnosed lung or colon cancer, 10 more changes [have occurred] in that cell already. Targeting all of them is going to be very difficult."[54]

Another problem with immunotherapy drugs is that despite their relatively high cost of development, there is no guarantee that they will be effective. Just as radiation is useless against certain types of cancer, immune-based chemotherapy drugs will sometimes be ineffective. Herceptin, for example, did not cure many of the breast cancer patients in Slamon's clinical trial. Because of the possibility of such expensive failures, research into these drugs is often put aside. According to Sydney Welt of

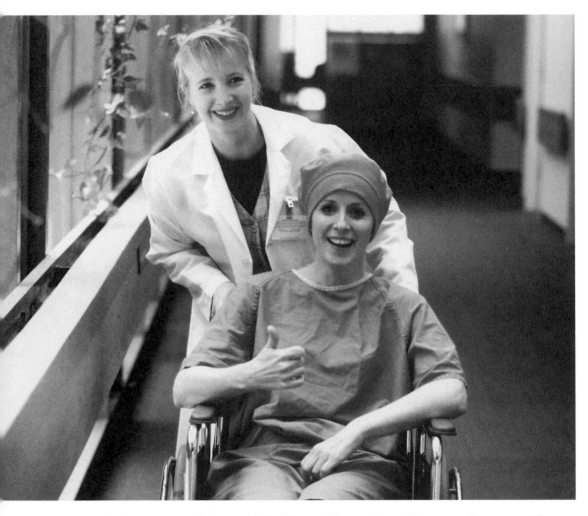

Recent developments in chemotherapy have given many cancer patients good reason to remain hopeful about the future.

Memorial Sloan-Kettering Cancer Center, "Some researchers have put promising antibodies on the shelf because producing large quantities for clinical-grade product costs too much."[55]

In light of these drawbacks, it seems unlikely that immunotherapy will become a stand-alone cancer-curing treatment in the near future. In fact, most cancer experts seem to think that the future of drug therapy for cancer is a combined approach. Ellen Vitetta, director of the Cancer Immunobiology Center at the University of Texas Southwestern Medical School, comments, "For cancer I don't think there will be any stand-alone curative therapy, whether it is antibody, chemotherapy, radiotherapy, or surgery."[56] By combining different approaches, doctors can take advantage of various mechanisms of action, in effect, bombarding tumors from many directions.

Magic Bullets Revisited

As research into chemotherapy progresses, doctors and researchers realize that cancer is too complex to develop a single magic bullet that is capable of curing every patient. It seems that the best course of action for ongoing chemotherapy research is to focus on small, attainable steps in improving treatment. Eventually, this approach will lead to a way to lower the death rate associated with cancer. "Someday," says Folkman, "we may treat cancer as a chronic, manageable disease, very much like we treat heart disease now."[57]

These small steps are working. Already remission times have grown from the scant few weeks that resulted from the initial nitrogen mustard trials to months and even years. According to Eugenie Kleinerman, an oncologist at the M.D. Anderson Cancer Center, "We're running a marathon, not a sprint. What's important is not how fast we run the first two miles but when we cross the finish line."[58]

The story of chemotherapy is a success story. Humans in search of a cure are no longer ingesting arsenic or coating their skin with donkey dung as they were five thousand years ago. Cancer patients are not forced to settle for an extra few days of life as they were when nitrogen mustard therapy was first introduced. Instead, modern chemotherapy drugs are effective and fairly safe and add years to patients' lives, sometimes even eliminating their cancers altogether. Although more chemotherapy research is necessary—as it is with every medical treatment—scientists get closer to a permanent solution for cancer every day.

NOTES

Chapter 1: The Search for a Magic Bullet

1. Quoted in Rose J. Papac, "Origins of Cancer Therapy," *Yale Journal of Biology and Medicine*, 2001, p. 392.
2. Quoted in Papac, "Origins of Cancer Therapy," p. 392.
3. Marie Curie, "The Discovery of Radium," address by Madame M. Curie at Vassar College, May 14, 1921. Ellen S. Richards Monographs No. 2. Poughkeepsie, NY: Vassar College, 1921.
4. Quoted in Rudolf Ludwig Karl Virchow, *Cellular Pathology as Based upon Physiological and Pathological Histology*, 2nd ed. Trans. Frank Chance. Birmingham, AL: Classics of Medicine Library, 1978, p. 27.
5. Quoted in "Paul Ehrlich: Pharmaceutical Achiever," Magic Bullets: Chemistry Versus Cancer, 2001. www.chemheritage.org.

Chapter 2: Poisons That Heal

6. Cornelius P. Rhoads, "Classics in Oncology. The Sword and the Ploughshare," *CA: A Cancer Journal for Clinicians*, 1978, pp. 309–10.
7. Louis S. Goodman, et al., "Nitrogen Mustard Therapy. Use of Methyl-bis(betachloroethyl)amine Hydrochloride and Tris(beta-chloroethyl)amine Hydrochloride for Hodgkin's Disease, Lymphosarcoma, Leukemia and Certain Allied and Miscellaneous Disorders," *Journal of the American Medical Association*, September 21, 1946, p. 2258.
8. Rhoads, "Classics in Oncology," p. 311.

9. Goodman, "Nitrogen Mustard Therapy," p. 2257.

10. Goodman, "Nitrogen Mustard Therapy," p. 2253.

11. Goodman, "Nitrogen Mustard Therapy," p. 2257.

12. Quoted in Papac, "Origins of Cancer Therapy," p. 394.

13. Murdoch Ritchie, "Alfred Gilman," *Biographical Memoirs V.70*. Washington, DC: National Academy Press, 1996, p. 66.

Chapter 3: The Early Arsenal

14. Quoted in Christine Bahls and Mignon Fogarty, "Reigning in a Killer Disease," *Scientist*, May 27, 2002. www.the-scientist.com.

15. George H. Hitchings, *Les Prix Nobel*, 1988. www.nobel.se.

16. Gertrude B. Elion, "The Purine Path to Chemotherapy," *Nobel Lectures*. Singapore: World Scientific, 1991, p. 447.

17. Quoted in Mary Ellen Avery, "Gertrude Elion," *Biographical Memoirs*, vol. 78. Washington, DC: National Academy Press, 2000, p. 20.

18. Charles Huggins, "Endocrine-Induced Regression of Cancers," *Nobel Lectures*. Amsterdam: Elsevier, 1970, p. 245.

19. Quoted in American Cancer Society, "The History of Cancer," March 25, 2002. www.cancer.org.

20. Huggins, "Endocrine-Induced Regression of Cancers," p. 238.

21. Huggins, "Endocrine-Induced Regression of Cancers," p. 245.

Chapter 4: The Problem with Poison

22. Quoted in Daniel Q. Haney, "Win-Win Situation: Armstrong's Cycling Win Is a Medical Victory, Too," *CNN/SI*, July 27, 1999. http://sportsillustrated.cnn.com.

23. Quoted in P/S/L Group, "Fatigue Most Prevalent, Longest-Lasting Cancer-Related Side Effect," September 22, 1998. www.pslgroup.com.

24. Quoted in "Cancer Specialists Turn to a Long-Ignored Side Effect: Fatigue," *New York Times*, April 10, 1999, p. A16.

25. Quoted in Adele Slaughter, "Rob Lowe Campaigns for Cancer Patients," *USA Today*, September 13, 2002. www.usatoday.com.

26. Quoted in Slaughter, "Rob Lowe Campaigns for Cancer Patients." www.usatoday.com.

27. Quoted in Slaughter, "Rob Lowe Campaigns for Cancer Patients." www.usatoday.com.

Chapter 5: Genetic Origins, Molecular Cures

28. Quoted in J. Madeleine Nash, "The Enemy Within," *Time*, September 18, 1996. www.time.com.

29. Arnold J. Levine, "Cancer Research in the 21st Century," *Keio Journal of Medicine*, 2001, p. 130.

30. Levine, "Cancer Research in the 21st Century," p. 131.

31. Quoted in J. Madeleine Nash, "Stopping Cancer in Its Tracks," *Time*, April 25, 1994. www.time.com.

32. I. Bernard Weinstein, "Addiction to Oncogenes—The Achilles Heal of Cancer," *Science*, July 5, 2002, p. 63.

33. Quoted in Jill Waalen, "Gleevec's Glory Days," *Howard Hughes Medical Institute Bulletin*, December 2001, p. 13.

34. Quoted in Waalen, "Gleevec's Glory Days," p. 13.

35. Quoted in Food and Drug Administration," FDA Approves Gleevec for Leukemia Treatment," press release, May 10, 2001.

36. Quoted in American Cancer Society, "Gleevec Also Nails Rare Gastrointestinal Tumors," May 14, 2001. www.cancer.org.

37. Quoted in Hal LaCroix, "Genetic Mutation Plays Key Role in Resistance to Gleevec: Discovery Will Guide Doctors in Customizing CML Treatment," *CBR in the News*, July 29, 2002. http://cbr.med.harvard.edu.

Chapter 6: An Alternative Approach

38. Quoted in "NOVA: Cancer Warrior," Public Broadcasting Service. Airdate: February 27, 2001.

39. Quoted in "NOVA: Cancer Warrior," Public Broadcasting Service.

40. Quoted in "NOVA: Cancer Warrior," Public Broadcasting Service.

41. Quoted in Nadia S. Halim, "Small Molecules in Large Proteins: New Class of Angiogenesis Inhibitors Shows Promise," *Scientist*, August 21, 2000. www.the-scientist.com.

42. Quoted in "NOVA: Cancer Warrior," Public Broadcasting Service.

43. Quoted in Harvey Black, "Angiogenesis—Promoting and Blocking—Comes Into Focus," *Scientist*, April 27, 1998. www.the-scientist.com.

44. Quoted in Mignon Fogarty, "Learning from Angiogenesis Trial Failures," *Scientist*, March 18, 2002. www.the-scientist.com.

45. Quoted in Fogarty, "Learning from Angiogenesis Trial Failures."

46. Quoted in Bahls and Fogarty, "Reigning in a Killer Disease."

Chapter 7: Smart Bombs

47. Quoted in Claudia Wallis, "Molecular Revolution," *Time*, May 18, 1998. www.time.com.

48. Quoted in Wallis, "Molecular Revolution."

49. Quoted in HealthTalk's Lymphoma Education Network, "Radioimmunotherapy: The Latest Advance in Lymphoma Treatment," December 7, 2001.

50. Quoted in Paul Smaglik, "Taking Aim at p53," *Scientist*, January 18, 1999. www.the-scientist.com.

51. Quoted in "The WCN Biotechnology Gene Therapy Symposium," May 18, 1998. www.wcnonline.com.

52. Quoted in Michael D. Lemonick and Alice Park, "Vaccines Stage a Comeback," *Time*, January 21, 2002. www.time.com.

53. Quoted in Lemonick and Park, "Vaccines Stage a Comeback."

54. Quoted in Bahls and Fogarty, "Reigning in a Killer Disease."

55. Quoted in Nadia S. Halim, "Monoclonal Antibodies: A 25-Year Roller Coaster Ride," *Scientist*, February 21, 2000. www.the-scientist.com.

56. Quoted in Halim, "Monoclonal Antibodies: A 25-Year Roller Coaster Ride."
57. Quoted in Alice Park, "Closing in on Cancer," *Time*, May 21, 2001. www.time.com.
58. Quoted in Nash, "The Enemy Within."

FOR FURTHER READING

Books

Robert Bazell and Mary-Claire King, *Her-2: The Making of Herceptin, a Revolutionary Treatment for Breast Cancer.* New York: Crown, 1998. Discusses the discovery of the HER-2/neu gene and its function, the discovery of the HER-2/neu antibody and its ability to shrink tumors, the development of the drug Herceptin.

Sallie Astor Burdine, *Who Needs Hair: The Flip Side of Chemotherapy.* Bluewater Bay, FL: Saba Books, 2001. A personal account of the advantages and disadvantages of chemotherapy.

Robert Cooke and C. Everett Koop, *Dr. Folkman's War: Angiogenesis and the Struggle to Defeat Cancer.* New York: Random House, 2001. A source for biographical information about Judah Folkman and for learning about the role of angiogenesis in cancer.

Jordan Goodman and Vivien Walsh, *The Story of Taxol.* Cambridge, UK: Cambridge University Press, 2001. Explores the development of Taxol from the discovery of the Pacific yew tree extract through drug production.

John Laszlo, *The Cure of Childhood Leukemia: Into the Age of Miracles.* New Brunswick: Rutgers University Press, 1995. An account of the work done over the last century to increase the cure rate of children with leukemia; includes good information about George Hitchings and Gertrude Elion.

Steven Lehrer, *Explorers of the Body.* New York: Doubleday, 1979. Discusses milestones in the science of medicine, starting from ancient Egyptian times and including social and political issues that affected discoveries.

Michael Boris Shimkin, *Contrary to Nature.* Washington, DC: U.S. Department. of Health, Education, and Welfare, Public Health Service, National Institutes of Health, 1977. Explores the history of cancer research and the development of knowledge concerning cancer.

Arthur M. Silverstein, *Paul Ehrlich's Receptor Immunology: The Magnificent Obsession.* San Diego: Academic Press, 2001. Describes Paul Ehrlich's contributions to immunology and the treatment of disease.

Michael Waldholz, *Curing Cancer: Solving One of the Greatest Medical Mysteries of Our Time.* New York: Simon & Schuster, 1997. Evaluates research that has increased the understanding of cancer and how to cure it; focuses greatly on the researchers who are working to cure cancer.

Robert A. Weinberg, *One Renegade Cell: How Cancer Begins.* New York: BasicBooks, 1998. An account of the discovery of cancer from a historical standpoint.

———, *Racing to the Beginning of the Road: The Search for the Origin of Cancer.* New York: Harmony Books, 1996. Discusses the scientific breakthroughs in cancer research from a historical standpoint.

Periodicals

Artemis, "Attacking Tumors By Destroying Their Blood Vessels," December 2000.

Christine Bahls and Mignon Fogarty, "Reigning in a Killer Disease," *Scientist,* May 27, 2002.

Harvey Black, "Angiogenesis—Promoting and Blocking—Comes Into Focus," *Scientist,* April 27, 1998.

———, "The Goal: Control Blood Vessel Development," *Scientist,* March 18, 2002.

Mike Falcon, John Morgan, and Stephen A. Shoop, "Alonzo Mourning Blocks Anemia," *USA Today*, April 8, 2003.

Mignon Fogarty, "Common Denominators," *Scientist*, March 18, 2002.

———, "Learning from Angiogenesis Trial Failures," *Scentist*, March 18, 2002.

———, "The Reality of Targeted Therapies," *Scientist*, October 14, 2002.

Food and Drug Administration, "FDA Approves Gleevec for Leukemia Treatment," press release, May 10, 2001.

Christine Gorman, "The Hope and the Hype," *Time*, May 18, 1998.

———, "Rethinking Breast Cancer," *Time*, February 18, 2002.

Nadia S. Halim, "Monoclonal Antibodies: A 25-Year Roller Coaster Ride," *Scientist*, February 21, 2000.

———, "Small Molecules in Large Proteins: New Class of Angiogenesis Inhibitors Shows Promise," *Scientist*, August 21, 2000.

Tom Hollon, "Leaving Tumors No Way Out," *Scientist*, May 14, 2001.

Michael D. Lemonick and Alice Park, "Vaccines Stage a Comeback," *Time*, January 21, 2002.

Arnold J. Levine, "Cancer Research in the 21st Century," *Keio Journal of Medicine*, 2001.

Ricki Lewis, "From Basic Research to Cancer Drug: The Story of Cisplatin," *Scientist*, July 5, 1999.

———, "Herceptin Earns Recognition in Breast Cancer Arsenal," *Scientist*, April 30, 2001.

———, "The Return of Thalidomide," *Scientist*, January 22, 2001.

Mary Ann Little, "Hope for Childhood Cancers," *HealthState: The Magazine of the University of Medicine and Dentistry of New Jersey*, Spring/Summer 2000.

Thomas Maeder, "Frogs, Sharks, and Michael Zasloff: Nature Never Lies, But You Have to Ask the Right Questions," *Red Herring*, December 2000.

Brendan A. Maher, "One Human Enemy Against Another," *Scientist*, August 20, 2001.

Paul A. Marks, "The Conquest of Cancer," *Scientist*, January 18, 1999.

J. Madeleine Nash, "The Enemy Within," *Time*, September 18, 1996.

———, "Stopping Cancer in Its Tracks," *Time*, April 25, 1994.

New York Times, "Cancer Specialists Turn to a Long-Ignored Side Effect: Fatigue," April 10, 1999.

Kate Noble, "Bad Drug Makes Good," *Time*, January 26, 2003.

Rose J. Papac, "Origins of Cancer Therapy," *Yale Journal of Biology and Medicine*, 2001.

Alice Park, "Closing in on Cancer," *Time*, May 21, 2001.

Thomas Sancton, "The Ride of His Life," *Time*, July 26, 1999.

Dan Shaughnessy, "A Mystery Story with a Happy Ending: Even Dana-Farber Was Left Clueless," *Boston Globe*, May 17, 1998.

George W. Sledge Jr. and Kathy D. Miller, "Angiogenesis and Antiangiogenic Therapy," *Current Problems in Cancer*, January/February 2002.

Paul Smaglik, "Taking Aim at p53," *Scientist*, January 18, 1999.

Douglas Steinberg, "Closing in on Multiple Cancer Targets," *Scientist*, April 1, 2002.

———, "Varmus Discusses the Three Gs," *Scientist*, May 29, 2000.

Scott Veggeberg, "Fighting Cancer with Angiogenesis Inhibitors," *Scientist*, May 27, 2002.

Jill Waalen, "Gleevec's Glory Days," *Howard Hughes Medical Institute Bulletin*, December 2001.

Claudia Wallis, "Molecular Revolution," *Time*, May 18, 1998.

———, "The Rough Road to Recovery," *Time*, January 14, 1991.

Internet Sources

American Cancer Society, "Chemotherapy: What It Is, How It Helps," February 9, 2001. www.cancer.org.

———, "Gleevec Also Nails Rare Gastrointestinal Tumors," May 14, 2001. www.cancer.org.

———, "The History of Cancer," March 25, 2002. www.cancer.org.

———, "Survivor Goes from Bald to Glam: Anniversary Surprise Leads to Diagnosis," October 22, 2001. www.cancer.org.

Daniel Q. Haney, "Win-Win Situation: Armstrong's Cycling Win Is a Medical Victory, Too," *CNN/SI*, July 27, 1999. http://sportsillustrated.cnn.com.

Hal LaCroix, "Genetic Mutation Plays Key Role in Resistance to Gleevec: Discovery Will Guide Doctors in Customizing CML Treatment," *CBR in the News*, July 29, 2002. http://cbr.med.harvard.edu.

Magic Bullets: Chemistry Versus Cancer, "Paul Ehrlich: Pharmaceutical Achiever." www.chemheritage.org.

P\S\L Group, "Fatigue Most Prevalent, Longest-Lasting Cancer-Related Side Effect," September 22, 1998. www.pslgroup.com.

Adele Slaughter, "Rob Lowe Campaigns for Cancer Patients," *USA Today*, September 16, 2002. www.usatoday.com.

"The WCN Biotechnology Gene Therapy Symposium," May 18, 1998. www.wcnonline.come.

Websites

American Cancer Society (www.cancer.org). Contains a wealth of information about cancer and treatment options, as well as statistics and survivor stories.

Closing in on Cancer (http://rex.nci.nih.gov). Detailed time line of advances in cancer research and chemotherapy.

Magic Bullets: Chemistry Versus Cancer (www.chemheritage.org). Historical overview of cancer and chemotherapy and major milestones in the development of chemotherapy drug classes.

Neulasta.com (www.neulasta.com). Contains detailed drug information and survivor stories for patients suffering from neutropenia brought on by chemotherapy.

Procrit.com (www.procrit.com). Contains detailed drug information and survivor stories for patients suffering from chemotherapy-related anemia.

Broadcasts

"NOVA: Cancer Warrior," Public Broadcasting Service. Airdate: February 27, 2001.

Works Consulted

Books

Francis Adams, ed., *The Genuine Works of Hippocrates*, London: Sydenham Society, 1985. Hippocrates' works on medicine in translation.

Mary Ellen Avery, "Gertrude Elion," *Biographical Memoirs V. 78.* Washington, DC: National Academy Press, 2000. Biography of Gertrude Elion with a discussion of her work on purine-derived antimetabolites.

Paul Ehrlich, "Partial Cell Functions," *Nobel Lectures.* Amsterdam: Elsevier, 1970. Ehrlich's Nobel lecture discussing his theory of immunity.

Gertrude B. Elion, "The Purine Path to Chemotherapy," *Nobel Lectures.* Singapore: World Scientific, 1991. Elion's Nobel lecture discussing the development of purine-based anitmetabolites.

Charles Huggins, "Endocrine-Induced Regression of Cancers," *Nobel Lectures.* Amsterdam: Elsevier, 1964–1970. Huggins's Nobel lecture discussing the use of hormone therapy for cancer.

Constance M. Pechura and David P. Rall, eds., *Veterans at Risk: The Health Effects of Mustard Gas and Lewisite.* Washington, DC: National Academy Press, 1993. Discusses detrimental effects of mustard gas as a military weapon.

Murdoch Ritchie, "Alfred Gilman," *Biographical Memoirs*

V. 70. Washington, DC: National Academy Press, 1996. Biography of Alfred Gilman with a discussion of his work on nitrogen mustard therapies.

Rudolf Ludwig Karl Virchow, *Cellular Pathology as Based upon Physiological and Pathological History*, 2nd ed. Trans. Frank Chance. Birmingham, AL: Classics of Medicine Library, 1978. Describes Virchow's cell theory, which established that diseased cancer cells arise from other cells.

Periodicals

Marcia Barinaga, "Cancer Drugs Found to Work in New Way," *Science*, April 14, 2000.

———, "Designing Therapies That Target Tumor Blood Vessels," *Science*, January 24, 1997.

———, "Peptide-Guided Cancer Drugs Show Promise in Mice," *Science*, January 16, 1998.

Richard Bell, "What Can We Learn From Herceptin Trials in Metastatic Breast Cancer?" *Oncology*, 2002.

Isaac Berenblum, "Cancer Research in Historical Perspective: An Autobiographical Essay," *Cancer Research*, January 1977.

Bruce D. Cheson, "Radioimmunotherapy of Non-Hodgkin Lymphomas," *Blood*, January 15, 2003.

Paul Chinn, et al., "Antibody Therapy of Non-Hodgkin's B-cell Lymphoma," *Cancer Immunology and Immunotherapy*, May 2003.

Jennifer Couzin, "Smart Weapons Prove Tough to Design," *Science*, October 18, 2002.

George D. Demetri, "Identification and Treatment of Chemoresistant Inoperable or Metastatic GIST: Experience with the Selective Tyrosine Kinase Inhibitor Imatinib Mesylate (STI571)," *European Journal of Cancer*, September 2002.

Steven Dickman, "Antibodies Stage a Comeback in Cancer Treatment," *Science*, May 22, 1998.

Angelo DiLeo, et al., "Current Status of HER2 Testing," *Oncology*, 2002.

Brian J. Druker, "Imatinib and Chronic Myeloid Leukemia: Validating the Promise of Molecularly Targeted Therapy," *European Journal of Cancer*, September 2002.

——, "Inhibition of the Bcr-Abl Tyrosine Kinase as a Therapeutic Strategy for CML," *Oncogene*, December 9, 2002.

——, "Perspectives on the Development of a Molecularly Targeted Agent," *Cancer Cell*, February 2002.

Sidney Farber, "Chemotherapy in the Treatment of Leukemia and Wilms' Tumor," *Journal of the American Medical Association*, November 21, 1966.

Judah Folkman, "Fighting Cancer By Attacking Its Blood Supply," *Scientific American*, September 1996.

David M. Goldenberg, "The Role of Radiolabeled Antibodies in the Treatment of Non-Hodgkin's Lymphoma: The Coming of Age of Radioimmuno-therapy," *Critical Reviews in Oncology/Hematology*, July/August 2001.

Louis S. Goodman, et al., "Nitrogen Mustard Therapy. Use of Methyl-bis(beta-chloroethyl)amine Hydrochloride and Tris(beta-chloroethyl)amine Hydrochloride for Hodgkin's Disease, Lympho-sarcoma, Leukemia and Certain Allied and Miscellaneous Disorders," *Journal of the American Medical Association*, September 21, 1946.

Mercedes E. Gorre, et al., "Clinical Resistance to STI-571 Cancer Therapy Caused by BCR-ABL Gene Mutation or Amplification," *Science*, June 21, 2001.

Antonio J. Grillo-Lopez, "Zevalin: The First Radio-immunotherapy Approved for the Treatment of Lymphoma," *Expert Review of Anticancer Therapy*, October 2002.

John D. Hainsworth, "Monoclonal Antibody Therapy in Lymphoid Malignancies," *Oncologist*, 2000.

Ester M. Hammond, et al., "Antiangiogenic Therapy and p53," *Science*, July 26, 2002.

Kelly K. Hunt and Stephan A. Vorburger, "Hurdles and Hopes for Cancer Treatment," *Science*, July 19, 2002.

Thomas F. Imperiale, "Aspirin and the Prevention of Colorectal Cancer," *New England Journal of Medicine*, March 6, 2003.

Heikki Joensuu, et al., "Management of Malignant Gastrointestinal Stromal Tumours," *Lancet Oncology*, November 2002.

Malik E. Juweid, "Radioimmunotherapy of B-Cell Non-Hodgkin's Lymphoma: From Clinical Trials to Clinical Practice," *Journal of Nuclear Medicine*, November 2002.

Pavel G. Komarov, et al., "A Chemical Inhibitor of p53 That Protects Mice from the Side Effects of Cancer Therapy," *Science*, September 10, 1999.

Eliot Marshall, "The Power of the Front Page of *The New York Times*," *Science*, May 15, 1998.

Jean Marx, "Why Some Leukemia Cells Resist STI-571," *Science*, June 22, 2001.

Michael J. Mauro, et al., "STI571: A Paradigm of New Agents for Cancer Therapeutics," *Journal of Clinical Oncology*, January 1, 2002.

Graham Molineux, "Pegfilgrastim: Using Pegylation Technology to Improve Neutropenia Support in Cancer Patients," *Anticancer Drugs*, April 2003.

New England Journal of Medicine, "Looking Back on the Millennium in Medicine," January 6, 2000.

New York Times, "Cancer Specialists Turn to a Long-Ignored Side Effect: Fatigue," April 10, 1999.

Robert Laing Noble, "The Discovery of the Vinca Alkaloids—Chemotherapeutic Agents Against Cancer," *Biochemistry and Cell Biology*, December 1990.

Michael O'Dwyer and Brian J. Druker, "STI571: An Inhibitor of the BCR-ABL Tyrosine Kinase for the Treatment of Chronic Myelogenous Leukaemia," *Lancet Oncology*, December 2000.

Elizabeth Pennisi, "Training Viruses to Attack Cancers," *Science*, November 13, 1998.

Tonse N.K. Raju, "The Nobel Chronicles," *Lancet*, March 18, 2000.

Marie Ranson and Mark X. Sliwkowski, "Perspectives on Anti-HER Monoclonal Antibodies," *Oncology*, 2002.

Barnett Rosenberg, "Noble Metal Complexes in Cancer Chemotherapy," *Advances in Experimental Medicine and Biology*, 1977.

———, "Platinum Complexes for the Treatment of Cancer," *Interdisciplinary Science Reviews*, 1978.

Cornelius P. Rhoads, "Classics in Oncology. The Sword and the Ploughshare," *CA: A Cancer Journal for Clinicians*, 1978.

Robert S. Sandler, et al., "A Randomized Trial of Aspirin to Prevent Colorectal Adenomas in Patients with Previous Colorectal Cancer," *New England Journal of Medicine*, March 6, 2003.

Ian E. Smith, "New Drugs for Breast Cancer," *Lancet*, September 7, 2002.

Gerald A. Soff, "Angiostatin and Angiostatin-Related Proteins," *Cancer and Metastasis Reviews*, 2000.

I. Bernard Weinstein, "Addiction to Oncogenes—The Achilles Heal of Cancer," *Science*, July 5, 2002.

Joanne L. Yu, et al., "Effect of p53 Status on Tumor Response to Antiangiogenic Therapy," *Science*, February 22, 2002.

Internet Sources

George H. Hitchings, *Les Prix Nobel*, 1988. www.nobel.se.

Broadcasts

HealthTalk's Lymphoma Education Network, "Radioimmunotherapy: The Latest Advance in Lymphoma
Treatment," December 7, 2001.

Audio Recordings

Marie Curie, "The Discovery of Radium," Address by
Madame M. Curie at Vassar College, May 14, 1921,
Ellen S. Richards Monographs No. 2. Poughkeepsie,
NY: Vassar College, 1921.

INDEX

PICTURE CREDITS

About the Author

Sudipta Bardhan-Quallen holds a bachelor's degree and a master's degree, both in biology, from the California Institute of Technology. Her writing interests range from nonfiction for young adults to poetry for children. She lives in New Jersey with her husband and two daughters.